BIRD BRAIN

CHUCK MULLIN

Contents

INTRODUCTION

Anxiety is a wild ride. Often, there seems to be an assumption that if you're mentally ill, you just sit around and cry all the time. There is a certain amount of that, true, but that's not all there is to it. Sometimes, I walk around and cry!

There is also a slew of complex emotions and experiences that accompany anxiety—nerves, fear, tentative happiness, the arduous business of forming human connections, the never-ending struggle to convince yourself that you deserve to be content, and so on—usually all experienced concurrently to form an unmanageable cocktail of emotional despair.

I first started experiencing anxiety when I was around seventeen, as the prospect of jetting off to university (where I knew no one except my then-boyfriend), and fending for myself, began to loom over me like a giant blimp full of killer bees. (Side note: Don't ever, ever, ever, ever, ever go to university solely to follow a romantic partner. It rarely works out well.) Initially, I thought I was undergoing a completely understandable case of nerves. Nerves that just permeated my entire being 24/7 and suddenly made me hate myself for every awkwardly strung together sentence that left my stupid, gross mouth.

The fact that something wasn't right began to hit home one evening when I went with my flatmates to the university's first freshers' night. As soon as I entered the campus club, it was like being submerged in water. I couldn't breathe. There were too many stimuli: too many bright lights, too much noise, and too many people. *Way* too many people, who I felt were all suddenly fixated on me, sneering at me, at how I looked, how I moved, how I simply existed. It's funny how anxiety makes you feel like you're simultaneously the most important and the most insignificant person in the room. I'd never experienced this tsunami of emotion before. I was probably standing in the entrance for all of a minute before I calmly walked out into the smoking area, hopped the security gate preventing people from sneaking in, and ran all the way back to my flat to bury myself under my bedcovers. I promptly cried myself to sleep. It was 10 p.m., and I had been at university for eight hours.

Over the next few years, I experienced a steadily increasing number of these episodes, not only in densely packed environments but also over the most inconsequential matters. I couldn't engage in basic conversation without feeling like I was sweating out my body's entire water content. The thought of having a social interaction I wasn't prepared for sent my heart rate into overdrive.

I tried to brave the doctor and counseling services, but it was almost as if there was a physical barrier preventing me from getting help. I had no idea where to begin if I attempted to talk about what I was going through—I didn't even know why the hell I was feeling this way in the first place. So I did what seemed like the only reasonable solution to this dilemma and kept all my feelings bottled up and squashed down in the deepest parts of my brain.

As a consequence of this repression, I became weirdly talented at presenting a well-adjusted persona to the world. I'd navigate through social situations with apparent ease, all the while internally screaming and looking forward to when I could get home and cry into my pillow. I think I told maybe three or four close friends about it, but only through rambling WhatsApp messages—never in person, unless I was absolutely shit-faced and couldn't keep the bad feelings in their bottles.

Eventually, despite feeling as though I couldn't hate my life any more, I graduated from university and became increasingly disillusioned with where I was headed. I felt stuck in a full-time retail position, in an incredibly wealthy area where basically every customer was an arrogant toe-rag constantly in "Can I Speak to Your Manager" mode.

I've always loved drawing, and so, to give vent to some of the internal pressure, I began doodling silly comics about the existential nightmare that was my life. I didn't have a working scanner or a working art program, so I took terrible

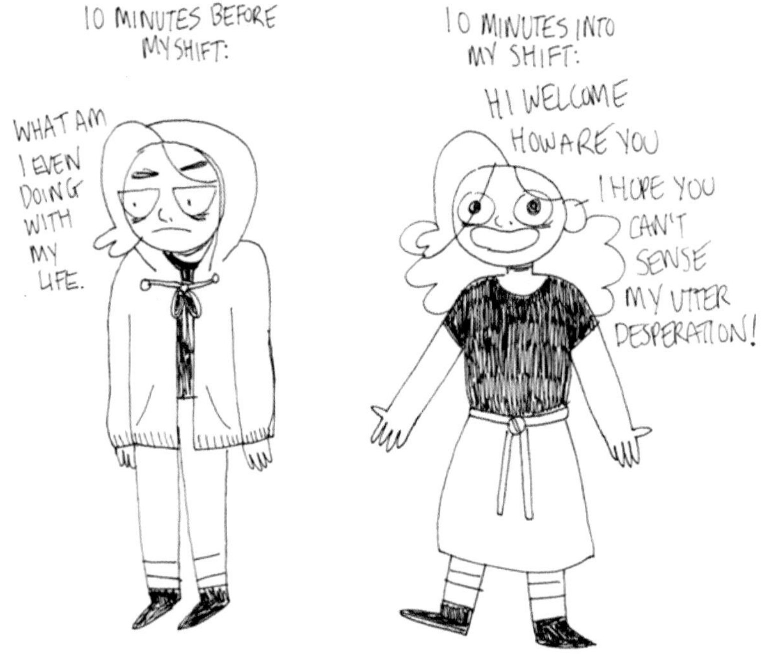
10 MINUTES BEFORE MY SHIFT:
WHAT AM I EVEN DOING WITH MY LIFE.
10 MINUTES INTO MY SHIFT:
HI WELCOME HOW ARE YOU
I HOPE YOU CAN'T SENSE MY UTTER DESPERATION!

quality photos of the comics to upload to Tumblr and then to a Facebook page I had created.

One day I was waiting to meet a friend in the town center and was idly watching a pigeon pecking at the floor. A middle-aged couple walked by and immediately started talking about how they hated pigeons, calling them dirty little rats with wings.

I've always loved pigeons; I find them cute and quirky and feel like they have an undeserved bad reputation. Pigeons used to be revered for their uses in sport and as messengers, and were a valuable source of food, but once better alternatives presented themselves, everyone just released their domesticated pidges en masse—that's why city areas are so densely populated by them. So it made me kind of sad to imagine a pigeon being able to understand this couple's insults and feeling terrible about itself. When I went home, I made a comic about it, and people seemed to really like it.

The positive reaction to this comic inspired me to start using pigeons to represent myself in all my future comics about mental health. It's weird, but there's something reassuring about projecting yourself onto something generally disdained and getting an encouraging response to it. You think that if people like this strange little depiction of yourself, then you in your entirety might actually be liked after all, despite your annoying brain trying to convince you otherwise.

You may also be wondering why I draw pigeons with floating eyes. The answer is because I think it's funny. Also, why not? Why does anyone do anything? Don't worry about it. It's all fine.

So, several comics and existential episodes after this decision, here I am writing this introduction. For this book. A REAL BOOK. That I went and drew and wrote myself. It's a bit surreal, and I am trying to play it cool, but my skeleton is ready to vibrate out of my skin with excitement. Thank you so, so much to everyone who has ever liked one of my drawings or sent me a lovely message—you are the reason I've been able to keep on doodling, and sometimes the reason I even bother doing anything. I wouldn't be here without you.

I hope you enjoy *Bird Brain* and that it helps you remember that no matter what you're going through, you're not alone. I also hope that you find some money in your pocket that you'd forgotten about, and that you see a really cool pigeon today. Thanks for picking up this book, I love you!!!

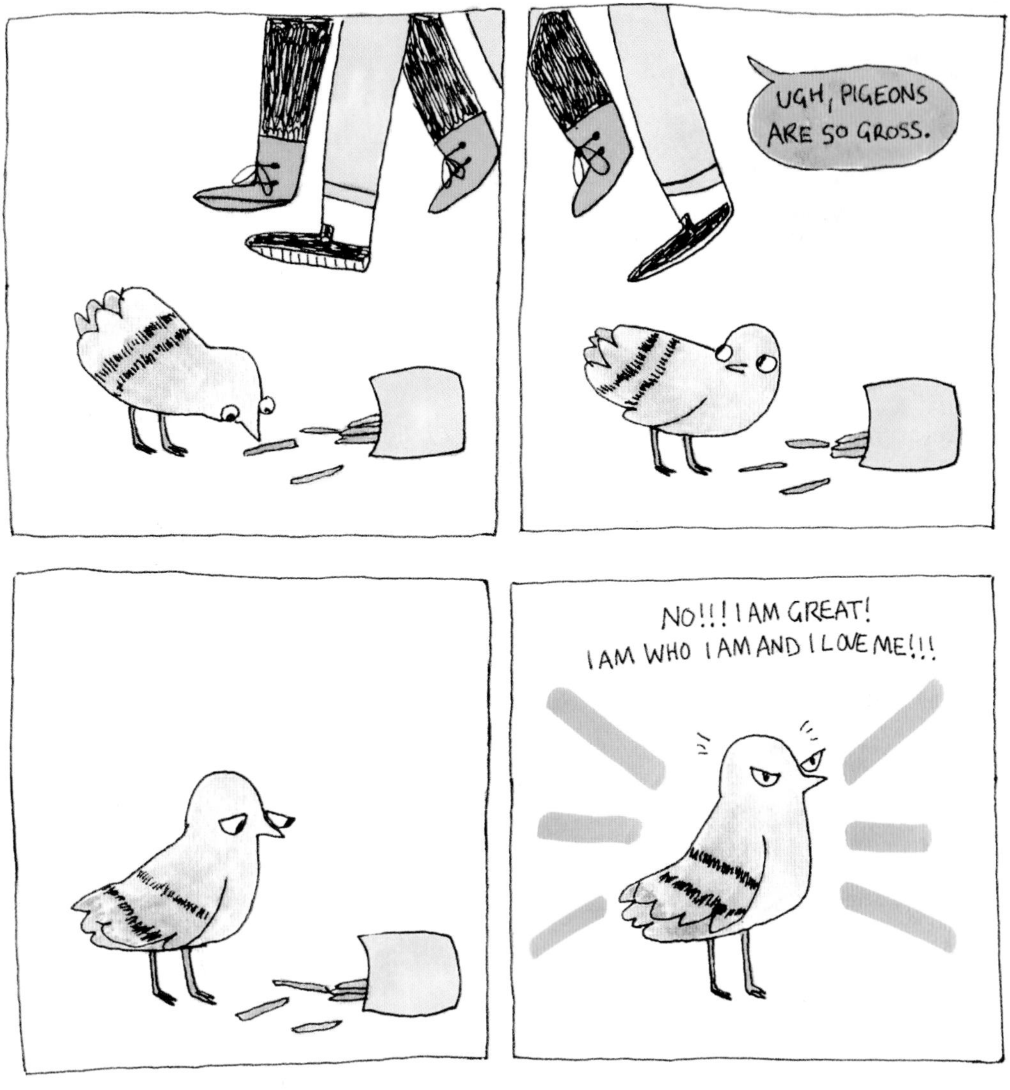
UGH, PIGEONS ARE SO GROSS.
NO!!! I AM GREAT!
I AM WHO I AM AND I LOVE ME!!!

BAD TIMES

The term "bad times" feels a little glib. Unfortunately, "times when I feel so utterly miserable and overloaded with panic that I completely detach from reality to retreat into a deafening void and wallow in self-deprecation for what feels like an eternity" just didn't have the same level of snappiness to it.

Typing the above sentence feels like I'm exaggerating how bad my mental health can get, but I'm really not. I used to think that being depressed or anxious just made you shy away under your bedcovers and sleep for hours, your brain reduced to a deflated balloon. And that is sometimes true; I wasn't surprised by this emptiness when my mental illnesses began manifesting. (Not that expecting it helped me deal with it in any way.) What blew me away was the sheer *abundance* of feelings, the excess of misery, paranoia, worry, self-hatred, envy, exhaustion, guilt, and so on and so on, all blurring into a disastrous cocktail. I felt like a perpetually whizzing blender, brimming with emotions that threatened to knock my lid clean off and splash everywhere at a moment's notice.

While that doesn't sound like it could get any worse, somehow it can and it does. It's not enough that mental illness straps you onto a never-ending nightmare carousel spiraling downward into hell; no, it also isolates you from everyone with a powerful sense of finality. Sometimes I go about my day feeling as if I'm encased in an invisible bubble. I seem completely fine, but in actuality, there's this tangible barrier physically separating me from the rest of the world. It absorbs anyone's attempt to probe beyond the surface and traps all my attempts to vocalize what's rattling around inside my brain, until I'm suffocated.

The bubble ignores rational thought. Logically, I know that I am not the only person going through this. Logically, I know that my loved ones would support me through anything. But mental illness takes any positive, factual thought you may have and Frisbees it into space. Without these gleams of optimism, you're left to force your way upstream against a raging river, alone, all the while blaming yourself for getting into this mess. *If only I had done this*, you think, *or this, or that, or any of those other five million options that have only just occurred to me, that I absolutely definitely would've 100 percent been able to do.* It feels simultaneously completely avoidable and totally inevitable.

So, yeah . . . it's pretty bad. I've never been good at getting the words to come out of my mouth to describe this. Art filters it out much more effectively, sucking all the negativity out of my brain like a leech and bleeding it onto paper.

Although I can never really draw something in the midst of a downward spiral or panic attack—it's pretty hard to hold a pen when you're nervously sweating out the Pacific Ocean—once the edge fades, I try to make a comic to purge the experience. I've always loved drawing, but it surprised me just how much creating these pigeon comics helps me; they've become my tether to existence, my voice when my mouth fails me. My self-improvement is also definitely related to the soothing numb of medication, but hey, everyone still needs an outlet.

And the connections art can bring! It's very bittersweet, just how many people have said they relate to these comics; it sucks that so many people have gone through the same slog of shit, but it's oddly comforting to know that, actually, I'm not alone in what I'm going through. And neither are you. The comics in "Bad Times" all took shape from moments of crappiness in my life, and they can seem quite defeatist, but I hope that their nihilism can burst through my invisible bubble and into yours to connect us. A strange sort of connection, but a connection nonetheless.

ANXIETY FEELS LIKE I'M CONSTANTLY...

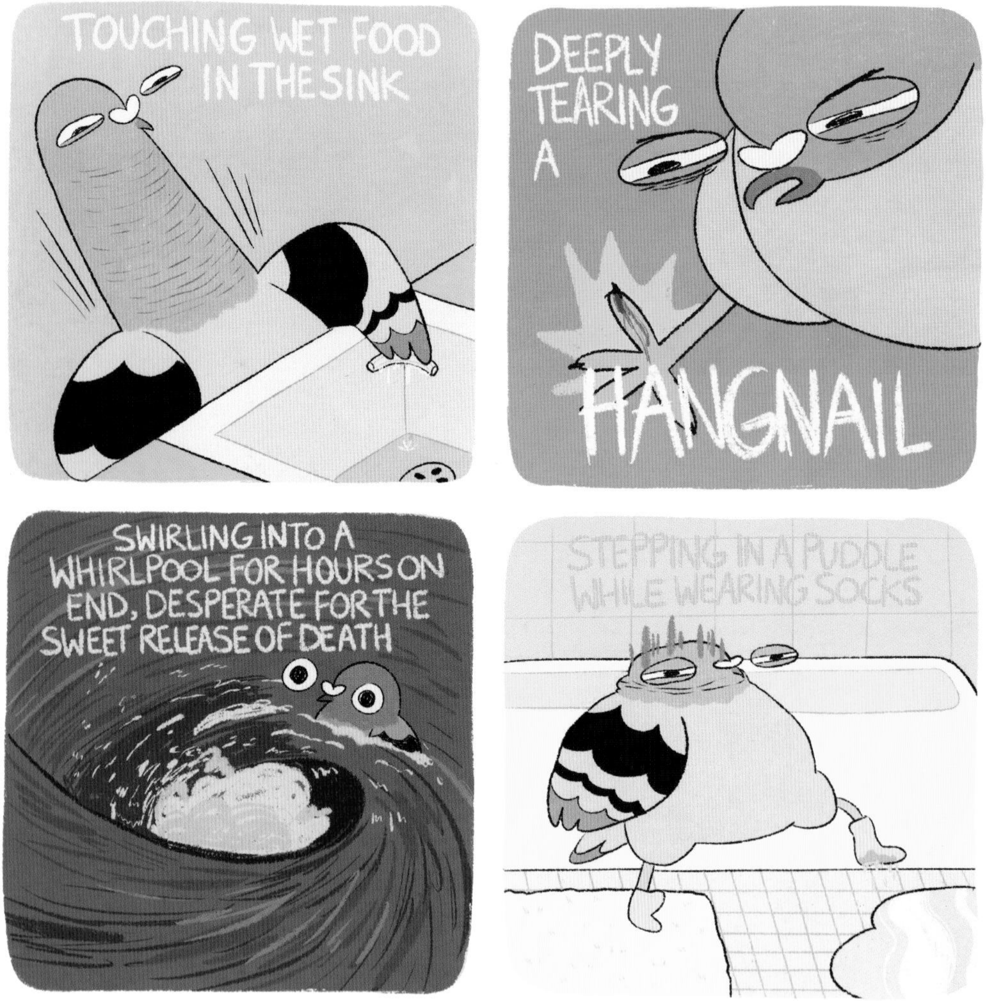
TOUCHING WET FOOD IN THE SINK
DEEPLY TEARING A
HANGNAIL
SWIRLING INTO A WHIRLPOOL FOR HOURS ON END, DESPERATE FOR THE SWEET RELEASE OF DEATH
STEPPING IN A PUDDLE WHILE WEARING SOCKS

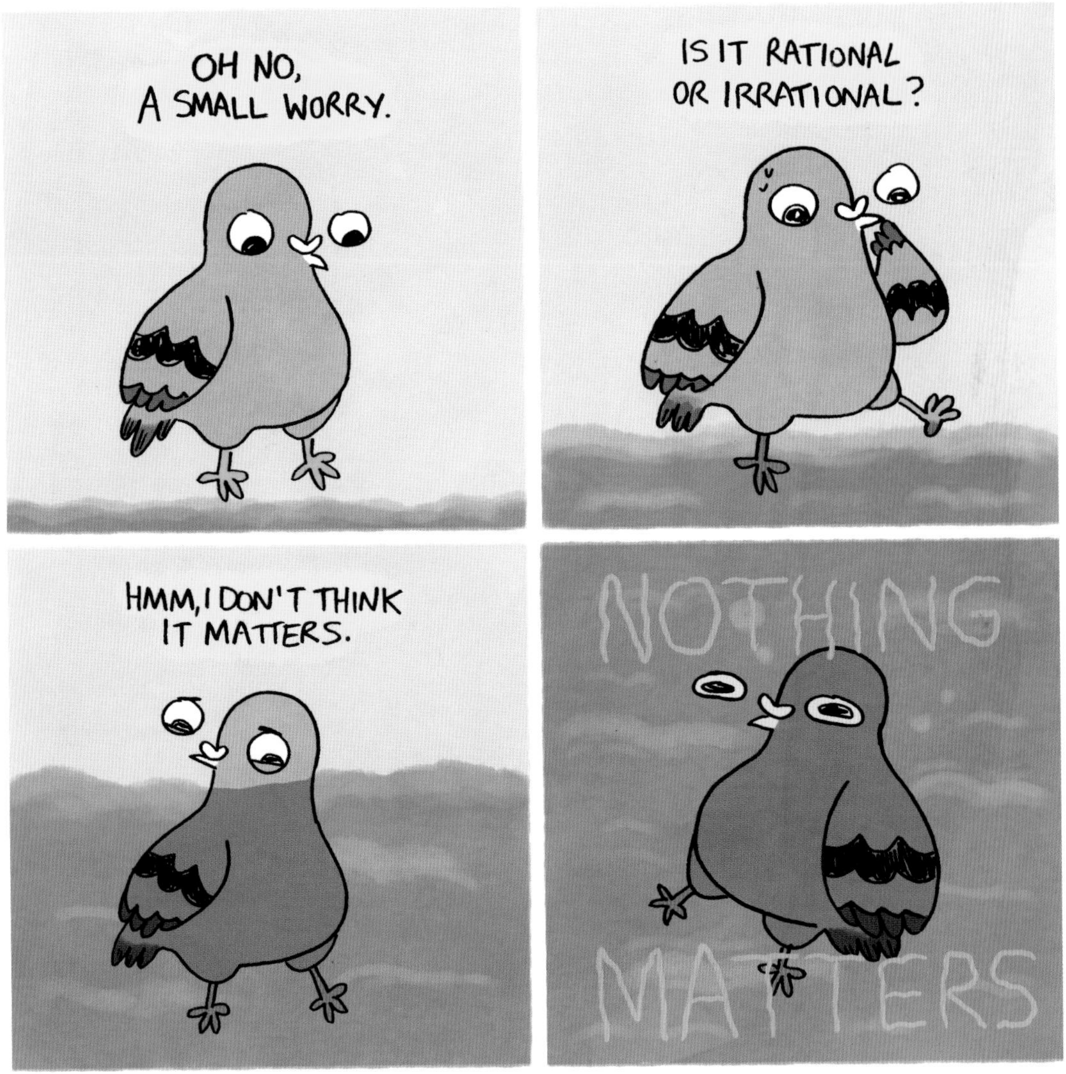
OH NO,
A SMALL WORRY.
IS IT RATIONAL
OR IRRATIONAL?
HMM, I DON'T THINK
IT MATTERS.
NOTHING
MATTERS

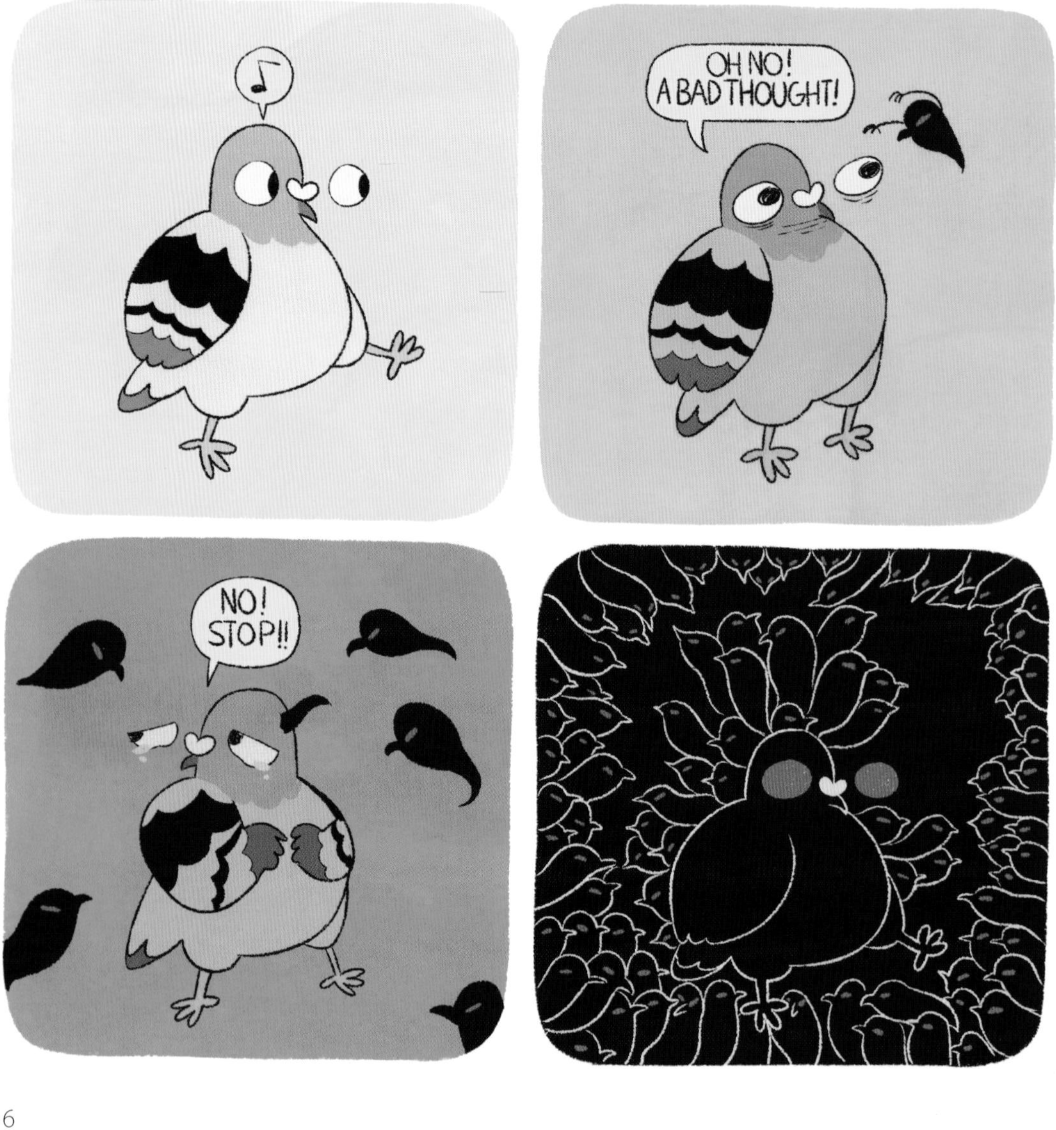
OH NO!
A BAD THOUGHT!
NO!
STOP!!

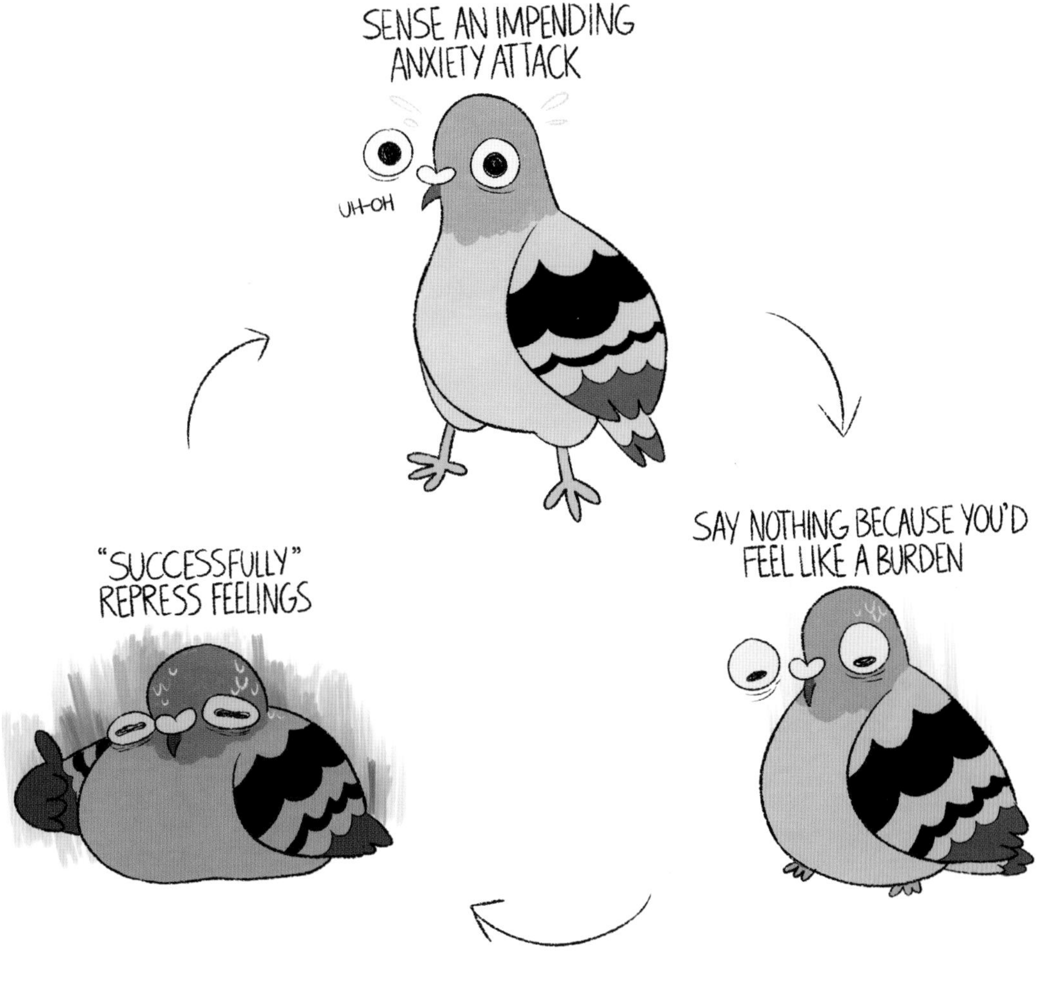
SENSE AN IMPENDING ANXIETY ATTACK
UH-OH
SAY NOTHING BECAUSE YOU'D FEEL LIKE A BURDEN
"SUCCESSFULLY" REPRESS FEELINGS

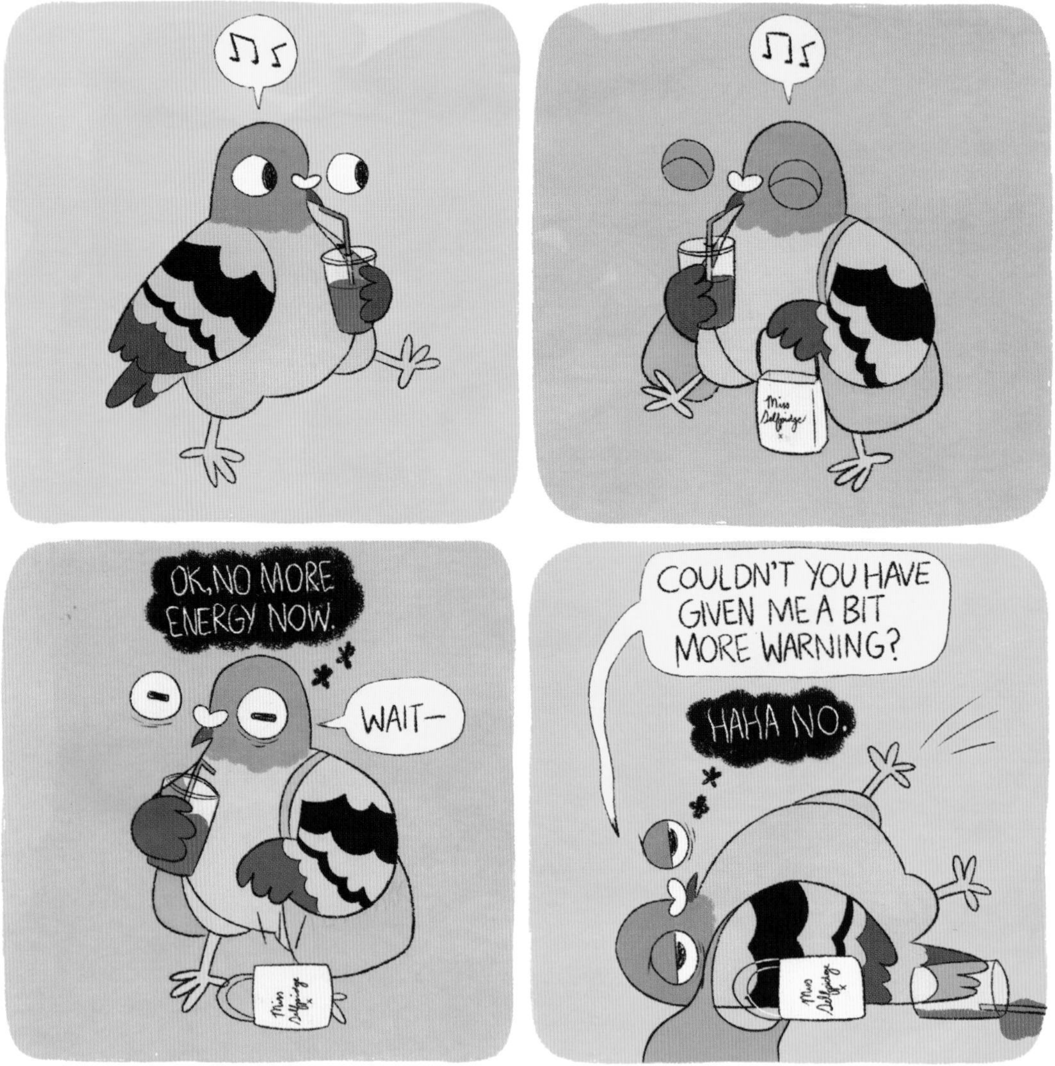
OK, NO MORE ENERGY NOW.
WAIT–
COULDN'T YOU HAVE GIVEN ME A BIT MORE WARNING?
HAHA NO.

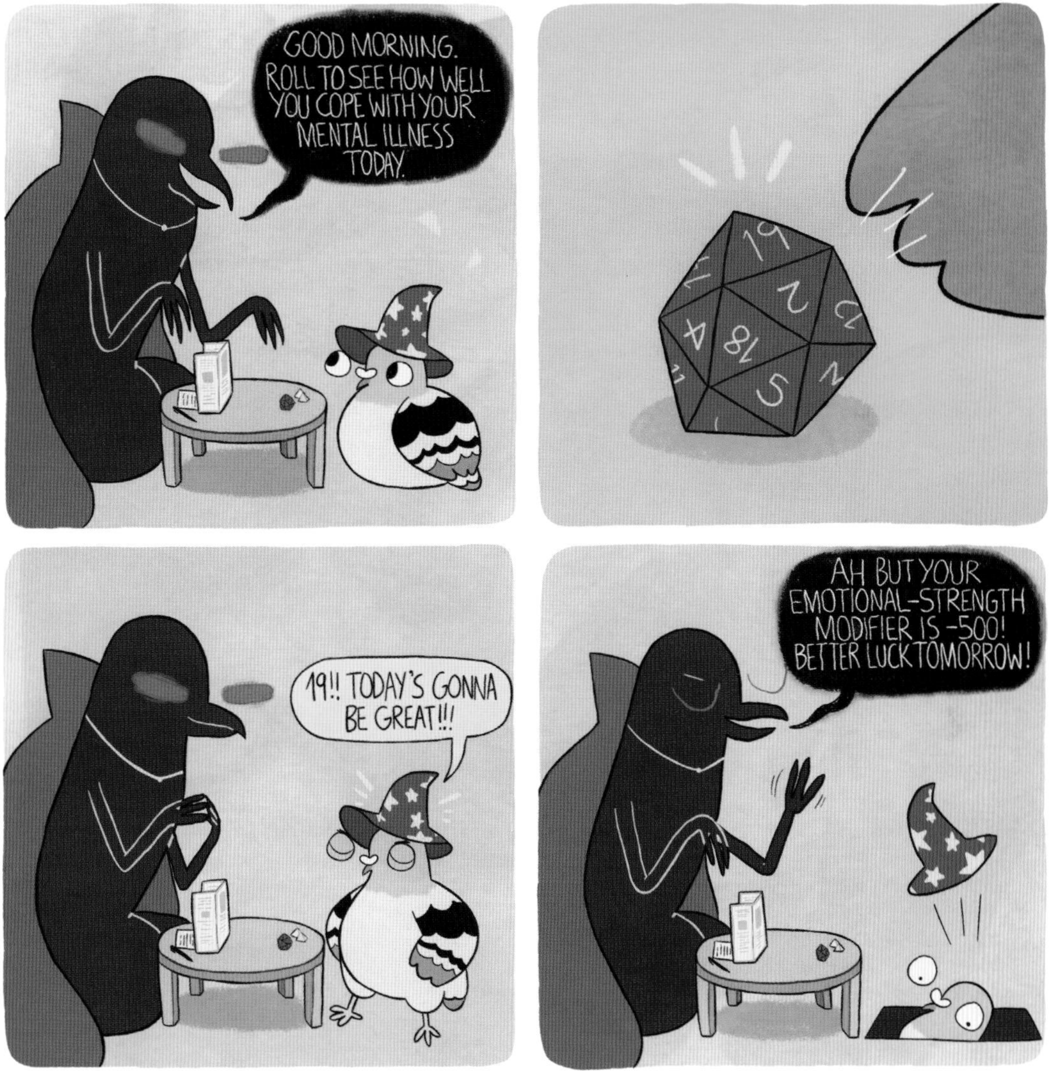
GOOD MORNING. ROLL TO SEE HOW WELL YOU COPE WITH YOUR MENTAL ILLNESS TODAY.
19!! TODAY'S GONNA BE GREAT!!!
AH BUT YOUR EMOTIONAL-STRENGTH MODIFIER IS -500! BETTER LUCK TOMORROW!

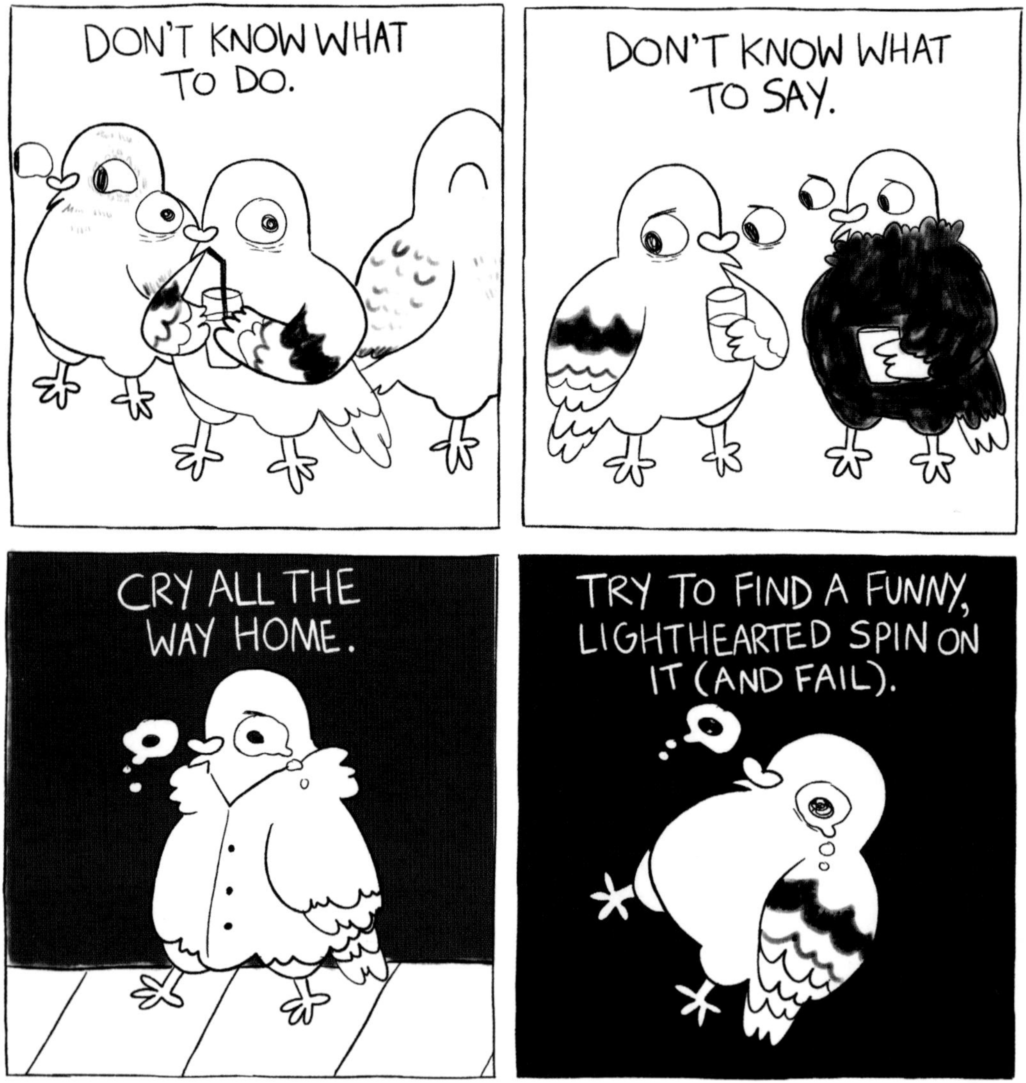
DON'T KNOW WHAT TO DO.
DON'T KNOW WHAT TO SAY.
CRY ALL THE WAY HOME.
TRY TO FIND A FUNNY, LIGHTHEARTED SPIN ON IT (AND FAIL).

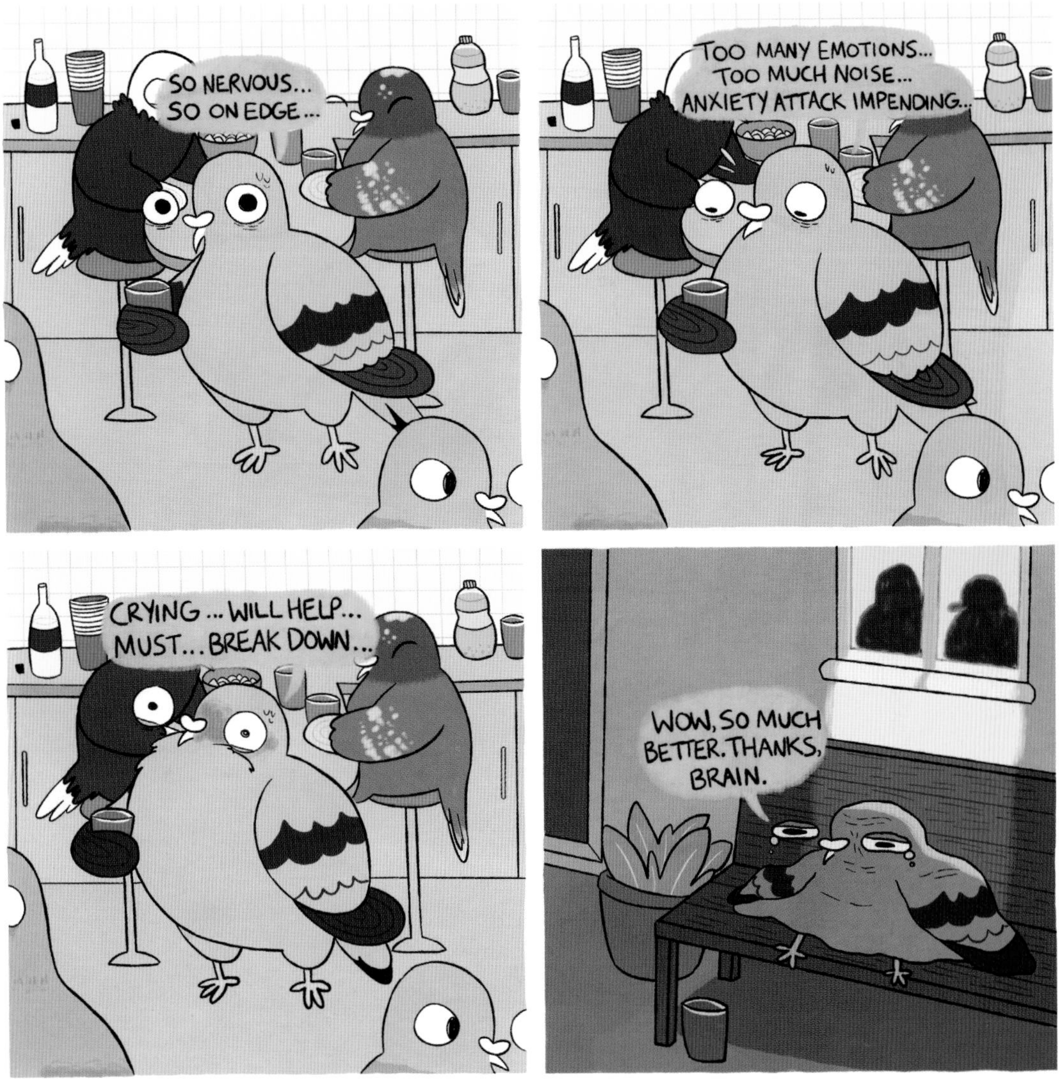
SO NERVOUS...
SO ON EDGE...
TOO MANY EMOTIONS...
TOO MUCH NOISE...
ANXIETY ATTACK IMPENDING...
CRYING... WILL HELP...
MUST... BREAK DOWN...
WOW, SO MUCH BETTER. THANKS, BRAIN.

These last two comics were based on the same awkward party experience and made within twelve hours of each other: the former, shortly upon returning home in a drunken stupor full of the flippancy that only vodka can bring, and the latter, the morning after, once shame and the hangover had kicked in.

I'm at a point now where I can deal with parties without wanting to disappear into a crack in the wall and become one with the insulation, but at my worst, large social gatherings just made me feel the emotional equivalent of being set on fire. It's either incredibly brave or incredibly stupid that I kept going to them.

An average schedule of my partygoing experience:

9:00 p.m.: Arrive.

9:15 p.m.: Complete greeting and catching up with the handful of people I know.

9:17 p.m.: Stand gawkily clutching a cup of fruity alcohol, staring at it like it's the most interesting thing in the world.

9:18 p.m.: Resolve to discover a conversation I can easily enter.

9:20 p.m.: Down my cup and refill.

9:23 p.m.: Introduce myself to someone.

9:24 p.m.: Quickly realize I have no idea how to participate in a conversation. *You moron. What did you expect? That you'd just be able to act like a "normal person"? Who the hell are you kidding?*

9:25 p.m.: Flush with shame as the other person breaks from my awkward eye contact and moves on to better prospects.

9:26 p.m.: Sear their look of disgust into my brain forever.

9:27 p.m.: Feel as if everyone's eyes are stabbing into me as punishment for this murder of an interaction.

9:28 p.m.: Everyone is talking to somebody else and having much more fun than they ever would with me, a fact they are screaming at me through osmosis.

9:30 p.m.: Feel sweaty and short of breath.

9:31 p.m.: Convince myself that locking myself in the bathroom and crying for a few minutes will expel all this negativity from me and leave me pristine. I am a dirty sponge that just needs to be wrung out.

9:32 p.m.: Queue for the bathroom.

9:40 p.m.: The queue for the bathroom has not shortened because the people in there are snorting coke off the sink. I've never done coke. Does coke calm you down? Is becoming a coke addict a viable form of self-care? Run back to the kitchen for any booze I can find.

9:41 p.m.: Concoct a cocktail that is 90 percent alcohol and 10 percent mixer. Immediately chug.

9:42 p.m.: Despair when this weirdly makes me feel worse rather than miraculously fixing all of my problems.

9:45 p.m.: Put my coat on and leave, silently heaving and crying the entire way home. Nobody notices or cares.

If I'm feeling particularly efficient, these events can be condensed into thirty minutes! Who says mental illness is a burden?

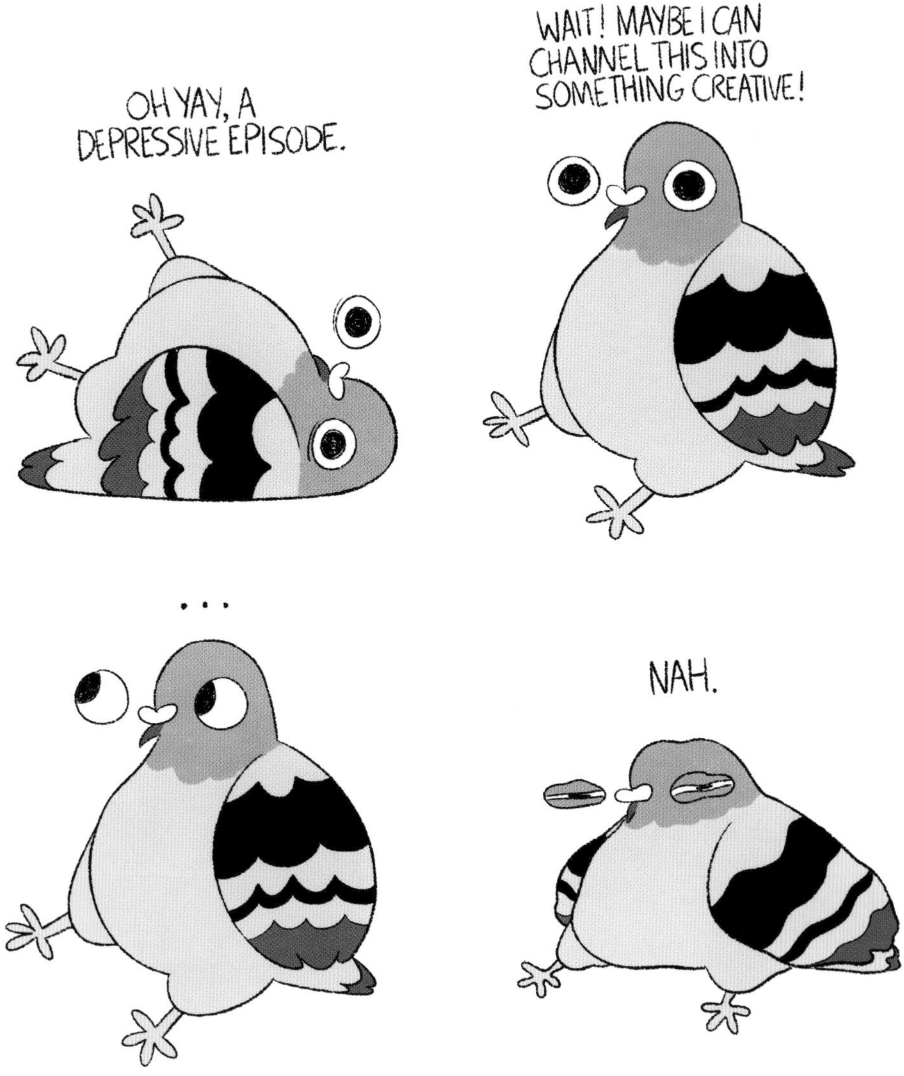
OH YAY, A DEPRESSIVE EPISODE.
WAIT! MAYBE I CAN CHANNEL THIS INTO SOMETHING CREATIVE!
...
NAH.

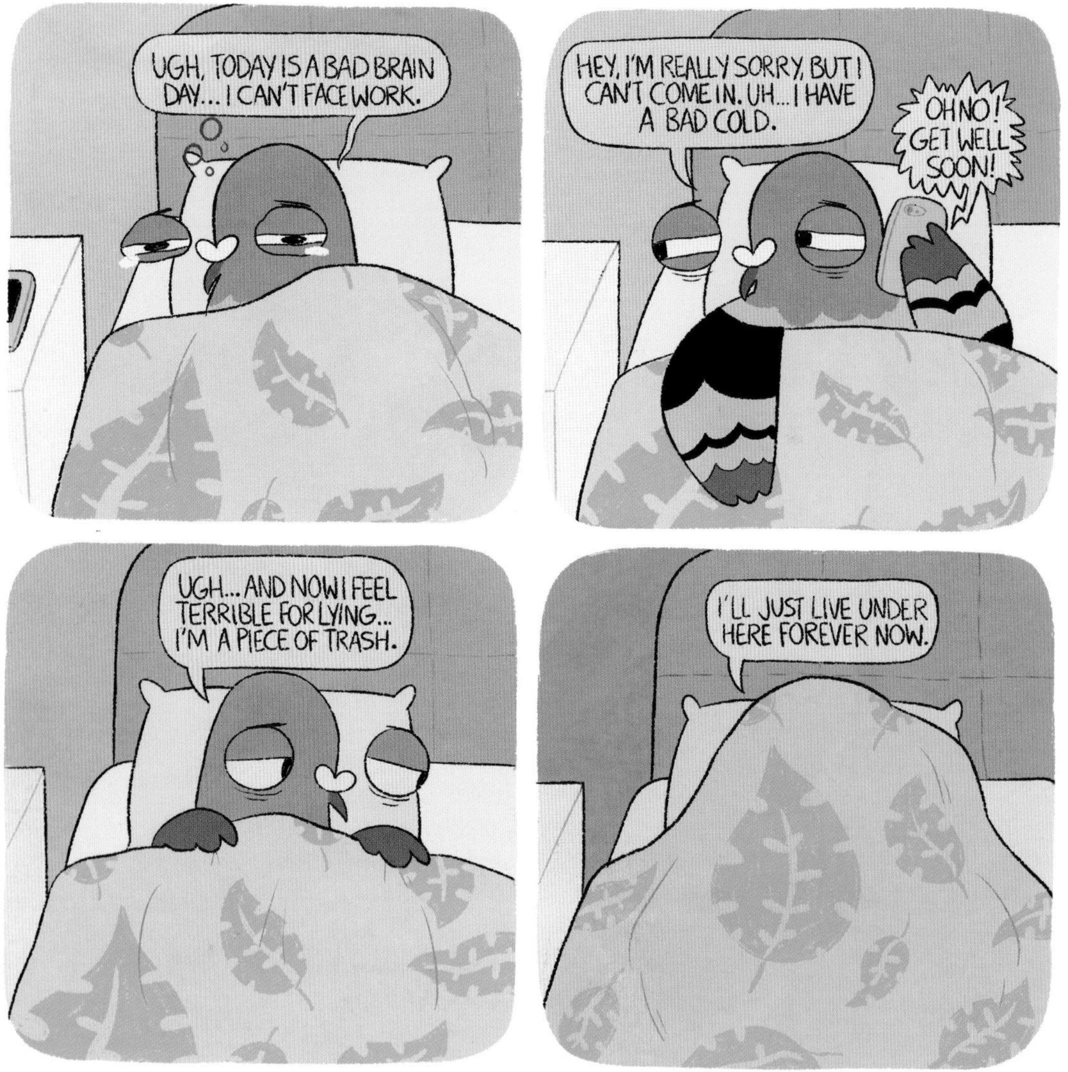
UGH, TODAY IS A BAD BRAIN DAY... I CAN'T FACE WORK.
HEY, I'M REALLY SORRY, BUT I CAN'T COME IN. UH... I HAVE A BAD COLD.
OH NO! GET WELL SOON!
UGH... AND NOW I FEEL TERRIBLE FOR LYING... I'M A PIECE OF TRASH.
I'LL JUST LIVE UNDER HERE FOREVER NOW.

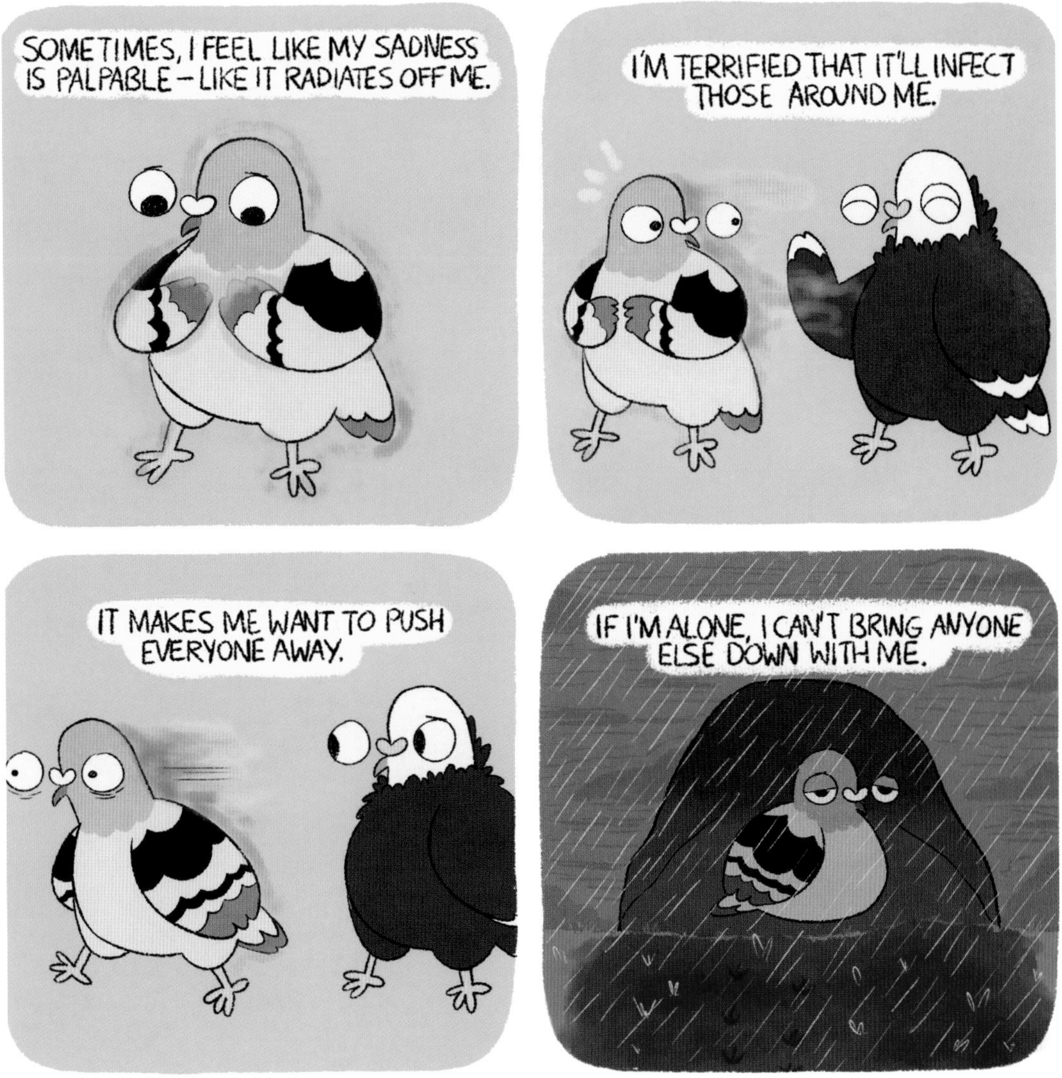
SOMETIMES, I FEEL LIKE MY SADNESS IS PALPABLE – LIKE IT RADIATES OFF ME.
I'M TERRIFIED THAT IT'LL INFECT THOSE AROUND ME.
IT MAKES ME WANT TO PUSH EVERYONE AWAY.
IF I'M ALONE, I CAN'T BRING ANYONE ELSE DOWN WITH ME.

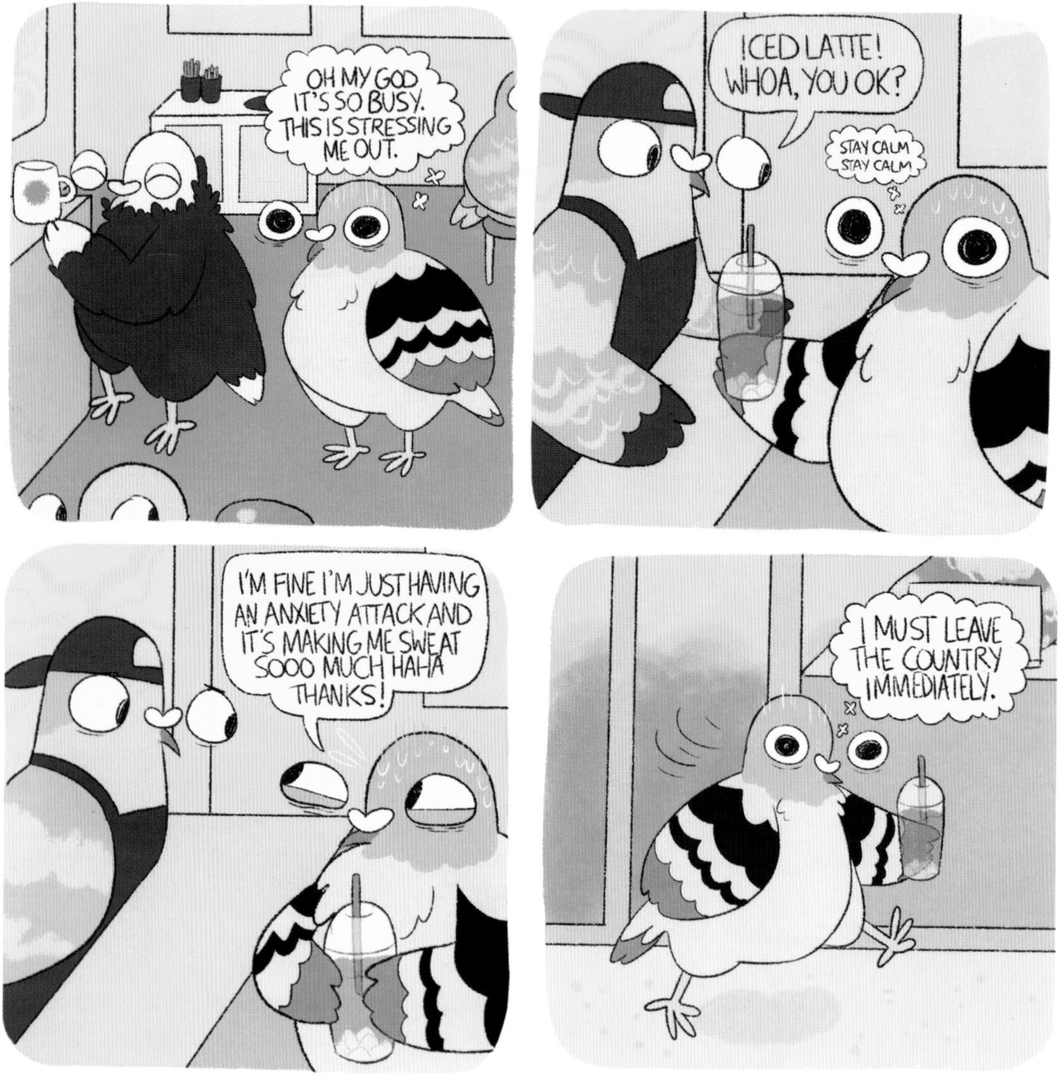
OH MY GOD IT'S SO BUSY. THIS IS STRESSING ME OUT.
ICED LATTE! WHOA, YOU OK?
STAY CALM STAY CALM
I'M FINE I'M JUST HAVING AN ANXIETY ATTACK AND IT'S MAKING ME SWEAT SOOO MUCH HAHA THANKS!
I MUST LEAVE THE COUNTRY IMMEDIATELY.

SOMETIMES I FEEL TRAPPED IN A BUBBLE, BLOCKED OFF FROM EVERYONE ELSE.
BUT THE THOUGHT OF BEING EXPOSED TERRIFIES ME BEYOND BELIEF.
AAAA SHIT

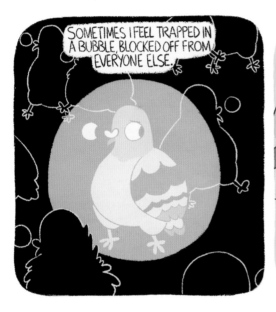

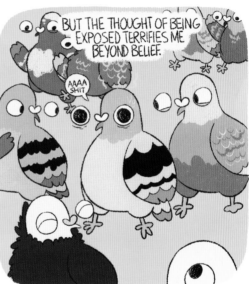

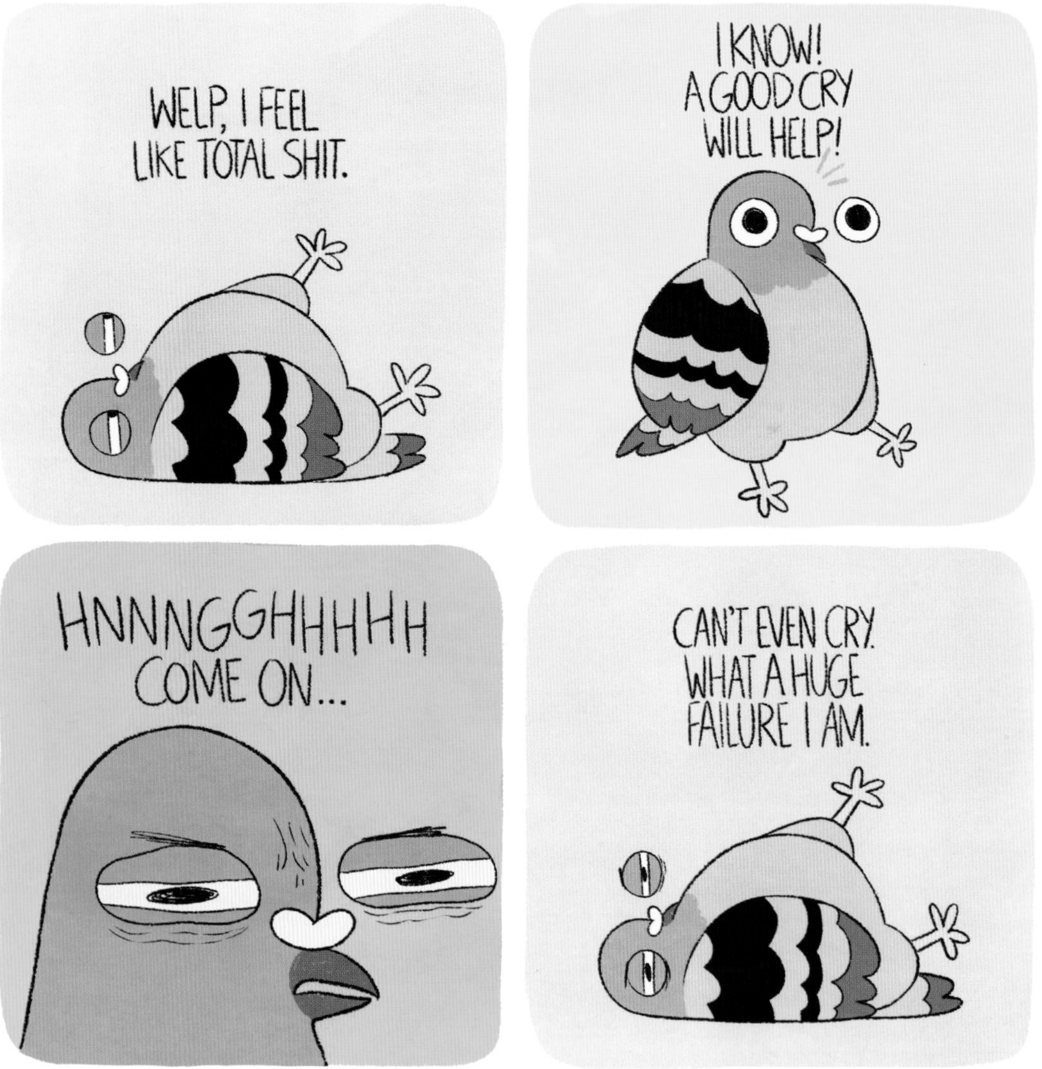
WELP, I FEEL LIKE TOTAL SHIT.
I KNOW! A GOOD CRY WILL HELP!
HNNNGGHHHHH COME ON...
CAN'T EVEN CRY. WHAT A HUGE FAILURE I AM.

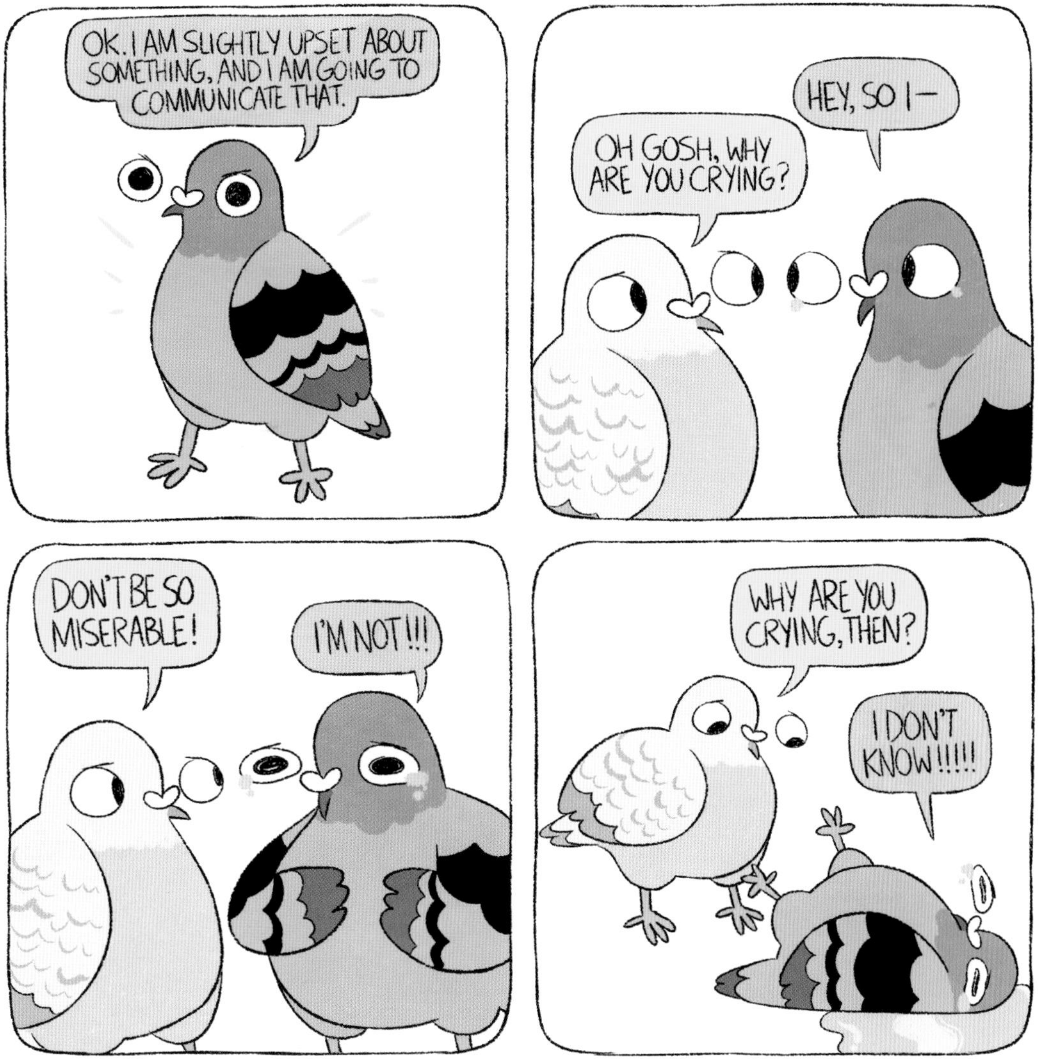
OK. I AM SLIGHTLY UPSET ABOUT SOMETHING, AND I AM GOING TO COMMUNICATE THAT.
HEY, SO I–
OH GOSH, WHY ARE YOU CRYING?
DON'T BE SO MISERABLE!
I'M NOT!!!
WHY ARE YOU CRYING, THEN?
I DON'T KNOW!!!!!

It's kind of funny how disproportionately my brain reacts to certain things. By "kind of funny" I mean "not funny at all but I search for humor in anything as a coping mechanism." One time I burst into tears because I'd worked a tough closing shift and just wanted some fries from McDonald's, only to discover that they'd closed due to a power failure. I was on the phone with my then-boyfriend when this happened and was inconsolable. I will say, however, that there is still a part of me that thinks this reaction was totally justified. Sometimes you just really, really need fries.

I truly believe that a good cry does wonders. It doesn't matter how insignificant the issue I'm facing is, I'm pretty much guaranteed to cry over it—but it helps so much. My emotions can sometimes run so intensely that I can't fully process what's happening—the only thing that will appease the burning despair bubbling in my belly is a long weeping session. Yes, purge all the negativity out through your tear ducts, that's it.

On the flip side, sometimes I can begin the process of a complete mental breakdown over being unemployed and unable to afford the cost of living, only to suddenly stop and fold all those feelings away like a freshly cleaned shirt. *Golly, that was a bit scary, wasn't it? Let's just pack all that away.* Sure is lovely to ignore your trauma. I am a ravaged husk of a human being, but it's totally cool.

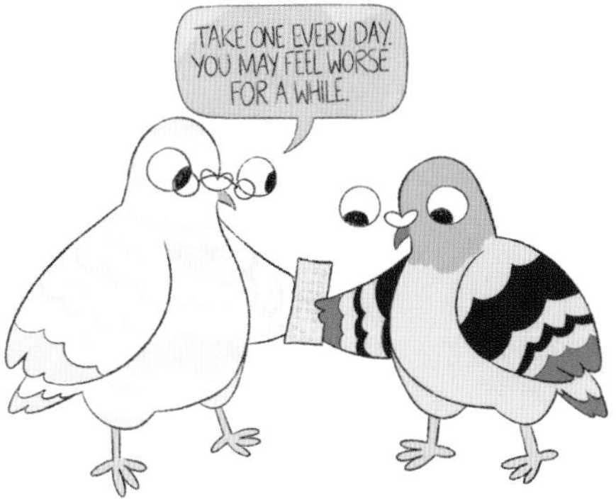
TAKE ONE EVERY DAY. YOU MAY FEEL WORSE FOR A WHILE.

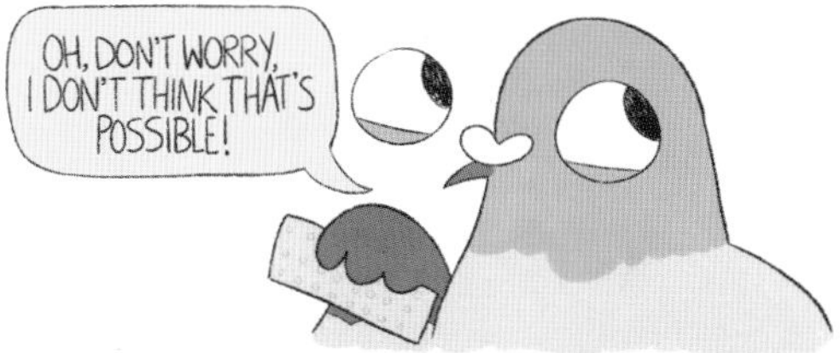
OH, DON'T WORRY, I DON'T THINK THAT'S POSSIBLE!

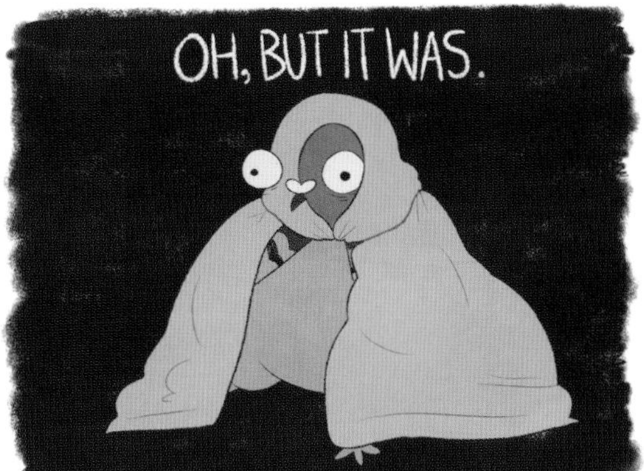
OH, BUT IT WAS.

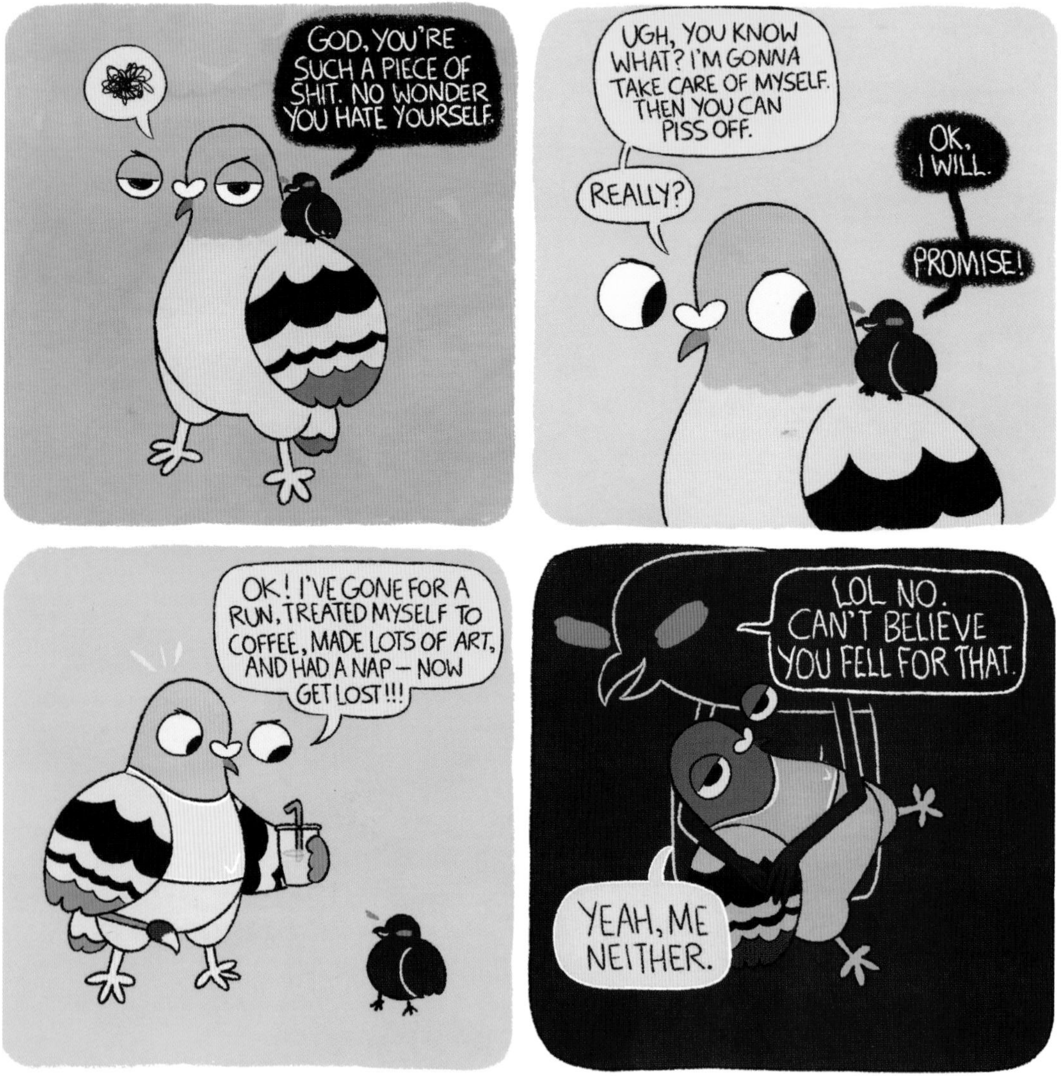
GOD, YOU'RE SUCH A PIECE OF SHIT. NO WONDER YOU HATE YOURSELF.
UGH, YOU KNOW WHAT? I'M GONNA TAKE CARE OF MYSELF. THEN YOU CAN PISS OFF.
REALLY?
OK, I WILL.
PROMISE!
OK! I'VE GONE FOR A RUN, TREATED MYSELF TO COFFEE, MADE LOTS OF ART, AND HAD A NAP — NOW GET LOST!!!
LOL NO. CAN'T BELIEVE YOU FELL FOR THAT.
YEAH, ME NEITHER.

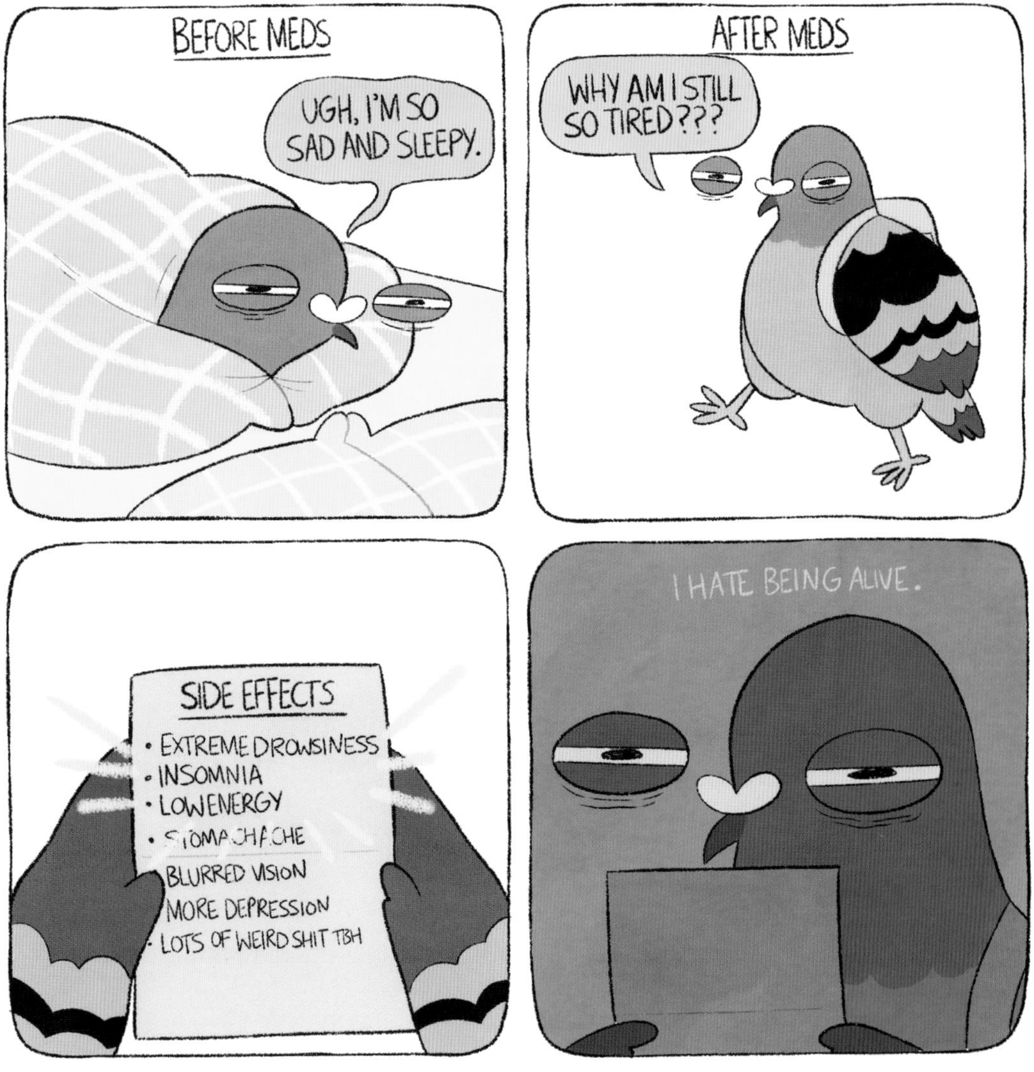
BEFORE MEDS
UGH, I'M SO SAD AND SLEEPY.
AFTER MEDS
WHY AM I STILL SO TIRED???
SIDE EFFECTS
• EXTREME DROWSINESS
• INSOMNIA
• LOW ENERGY
• STOMACHACHE
• BLURRED VISION
• MORE DEPRESSION
• LOTS OF WEIRD SHIT TBH
I HATE BEING ALIVE.

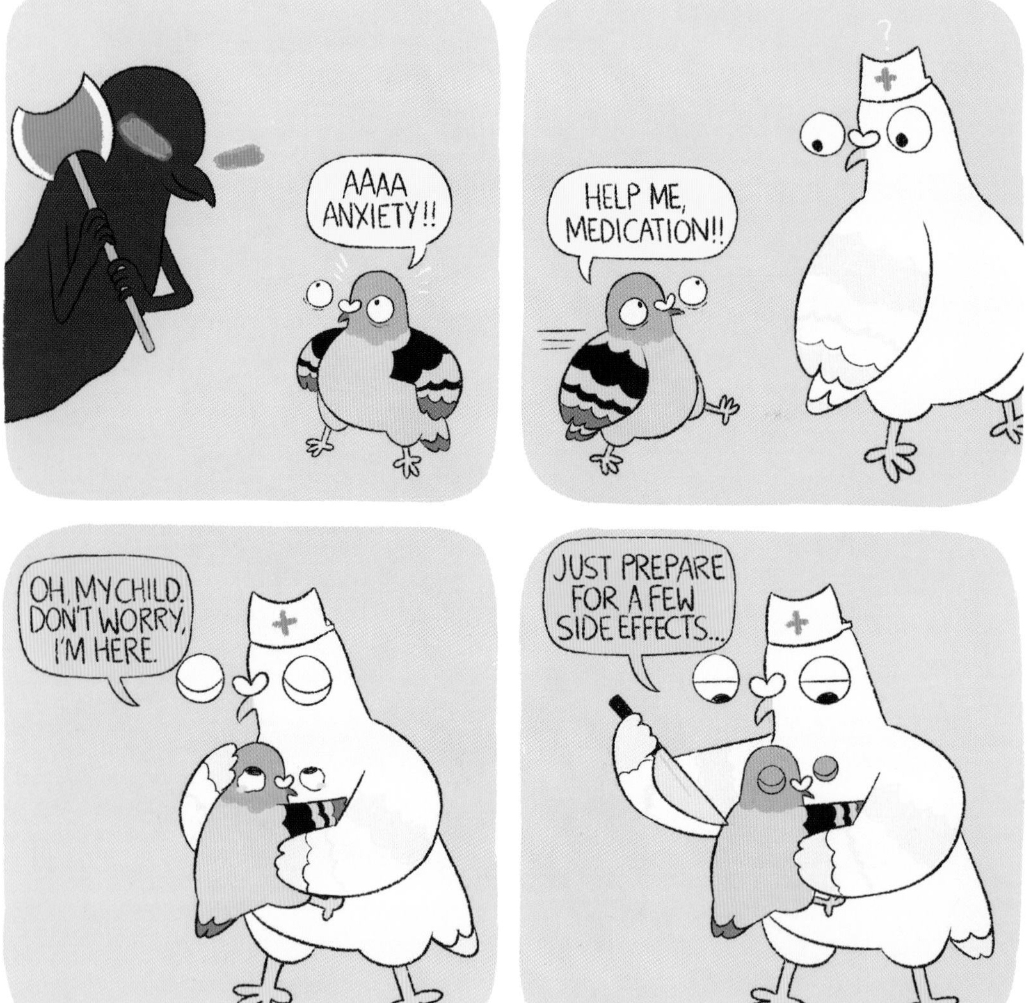
AAAA ANXIETY!!
HELP ME, MEDICATION!!
?
OH, MY CHILD. DON'T WORRY, I'M HERE.
JUST PREPARE FOR A FEW SIDE EFFECTS...

When I started taking medication for anxiety and depression, my doctor warned me that I may experience "some side effects." This turned out to mean "get ready for your body to go through a bunch of wild shit for a month or two."

For the first week, I couldn't sleep. The week after, I slept for fifteen hours a day. Fairly standard stuff. But then it was like my brain just started throwing darts at a wall of weird habits to select my next punishment. I began subconsciously grinding my teeth all the time, sometimes doing it so hard in my sleep that it woke me up. Then I went through a phase of feeling incredibly faint at random moments, like a delicate, bourgeois lady from the nineteenth century. I would sweat out liters, get unbelievable dry mouth, have ridiculously shaky hands . . . but then my body seemed to abruptly decide it had tortured me enough and rewarded me with delicious dopamine and a general sense of well-being.

From what I've gathered talking to others, my experience of side effects is on the mild side. I was very lucky to find the best medication for me on my first go; others go through this terrible rigmarole of side effects several times before they find the meds that actually work for them. Maybe my brain just felt sorry for putting me through a bunch of horseshit already and cut me some slack by responding positively to the first chemicals I pumped into it.

Although I complain about meds a lot, they've honestly saved my life, and I would definitely recommend them. They're not for everyone, though, so you should always discuss what's best for you with your doctor. Whatever that turns out to be, we can all agree that brains suck, and I can't wait to get my hypereffective skull circuit in the cyborg uprising.

MY TWO MOODS

AHHH OH BOY GOTTA GO FAST GOTTA DO LOTS OF THINGS WHAT THINGS? DOESN'T MATTER DO 'EM NOW QUICK GO GO GO AAAAAAAHHH!

AAH, MY OLD FRIEND...

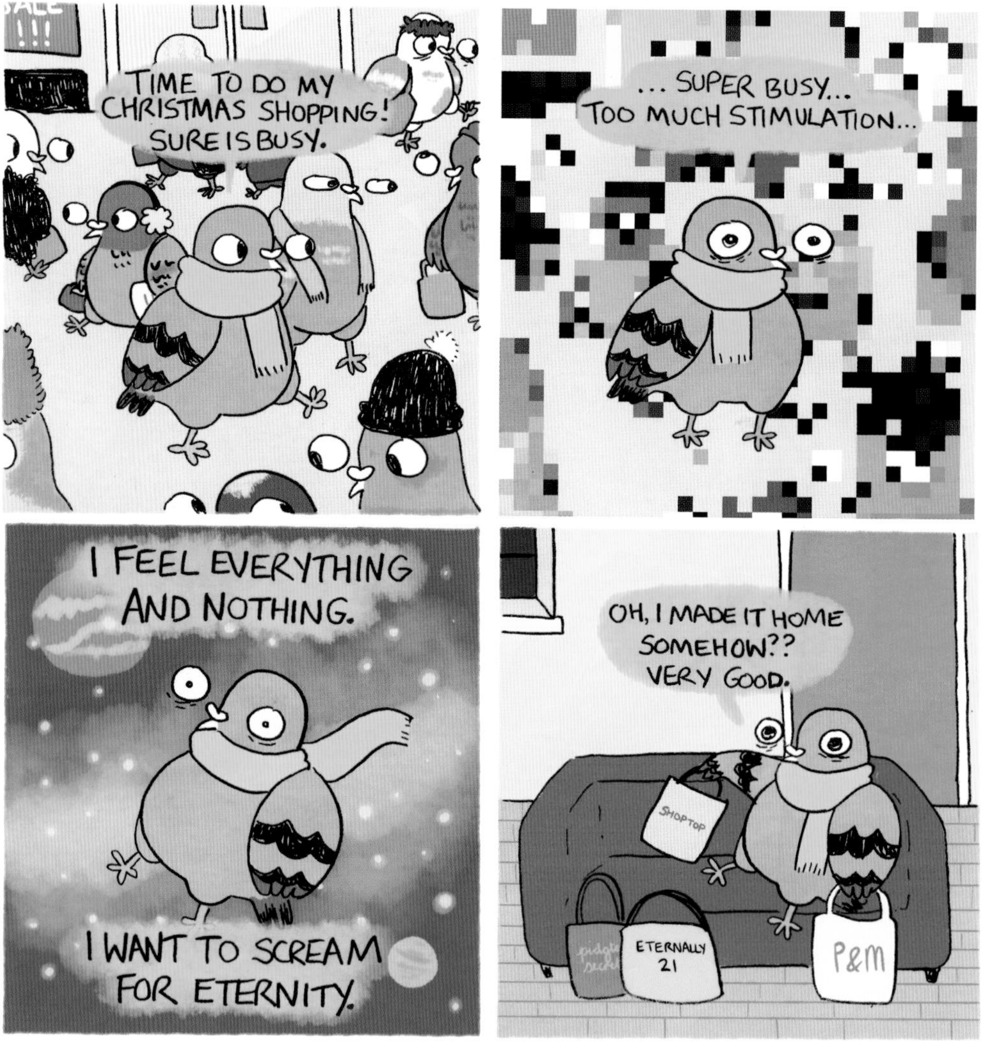
TIME TO DO MY CHRISTMAS SHOPPING! SURE IS BUSY.
... SUPER BUSY... TOO MUCH STIMULATION...
I FEEL EVERYTHING AND NOTHING.
I WANT TO SCREAM FOR ETERNITY.
OH, I MADE IT HOME SOMEHOW?? VERY GOOD.
SHOPTOP
ETERNALLY 21
P&M

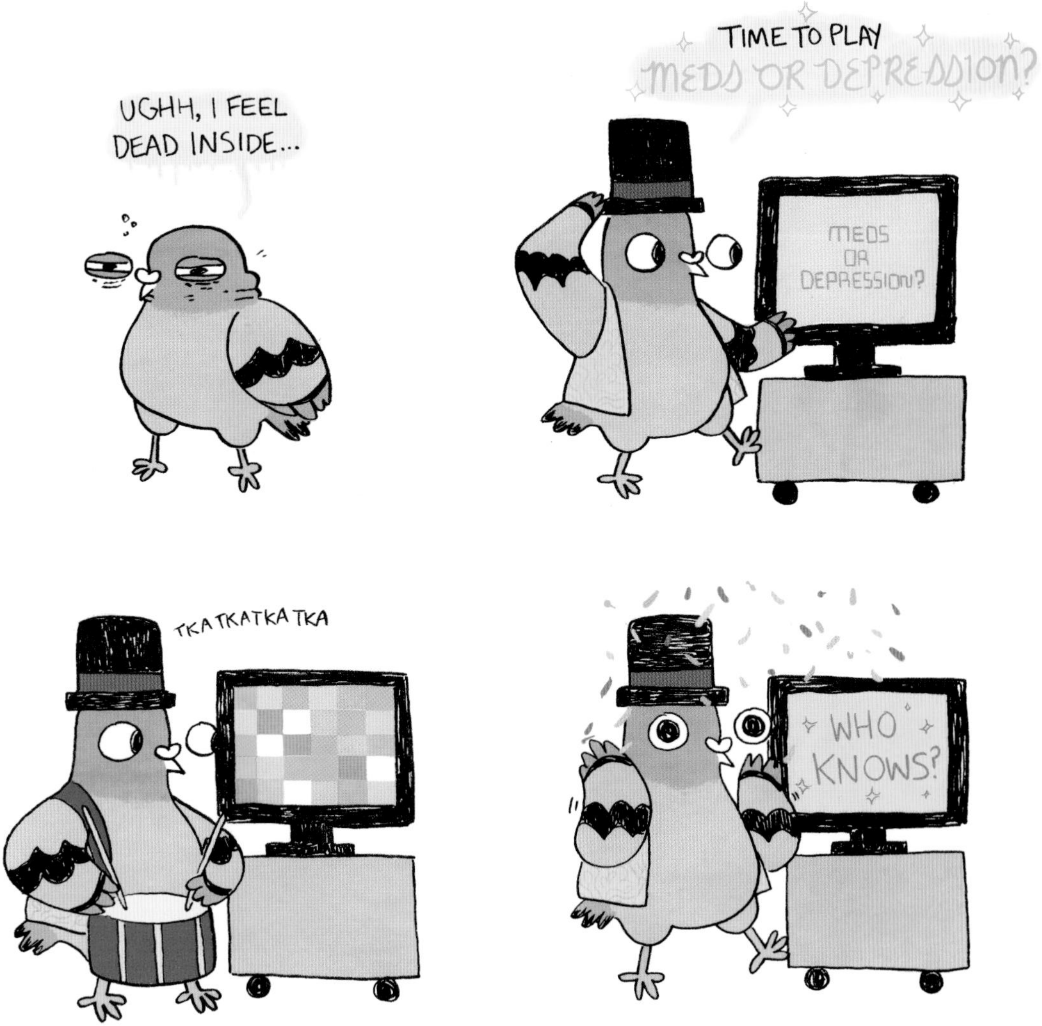
UGHH, I FEEL DEAD INSIDE...
TIME TO PLAY
MEDS OR DEPRESSION?
MEDS OR DEPRESSION?
TKATKATKATKA
WHO KNOWS?

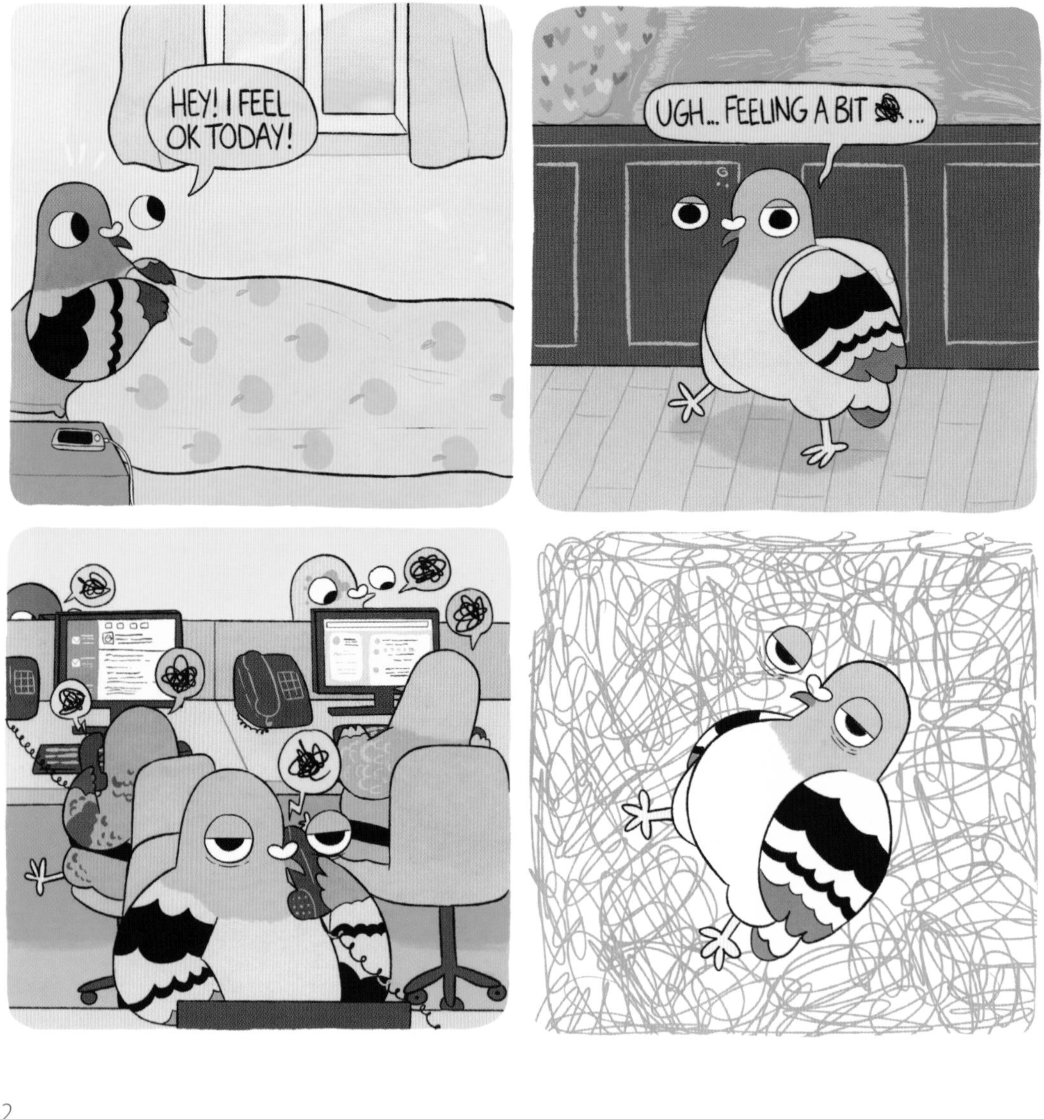
HEY! I FEEL OK TODAY!
UGH... FEELING A BIT ...

Quite appropriately, my memory of the first time I fully dissociated is patchy. Dissociation is a method of coping with extreme stress, where you feel like you're completely disconnected from yourself and your surroundings. Sometimes I think that sounds quite pleasant, to have a little break from myself, but in actuality, it's pretty horrific.

I remember that I was working a weekend shift in retail during the run-up to Christmas, and so we were slammed. Before I'd even started my shift, my nerves were shot just thinking about the chaos that I was about to endure. The day passed by in a flurry, and I ended up being so busy that my anxiety couldn't take hold. That was until about fifteen minutes before my shift was due to end.

I'd just cashed out somebody, who then asked my manager a question—something about using the staff toilets, I think? Anyway, my manager must've denied this woman's request, because she acted like my manager had just punched her teeth out. She utterly flipped out, calling us disgraceful, threatening to report us to our customer helpline, and so on: all the usual middle-aged, upper-middle-class white woman threats. At that point, even though I wasn't directly dealing with her, I just completely shut down. The day had proved too much for me. My brain decided *Yep, I'm done! You're on your own, kid!* It was as if I'd floated out of my body and was watching myself stand uselessly while this banshee put a curse on my manager. Before I knew it, I was halfway through my walk to the Tube station, wondering how the hell I'd suddenly gotten there.

Although it sounds quite nice to be able to detach yourself from a stressful situation until you're safely away, it was terrifying. I'd lost all control of myself, and now there was a huge gap in my memory. What did I do in that time? Did I say anything embarrassing? How did I manage to walk around without getting hit by a car, or getting lost? What if I hadn't come back to myself when I had? I didn't process these worries fully until I was under my bedcovers, curled up, and shaking.

I've only dissociated a few times, but each time has been horrible. Coming back to myself is always like being slapped awake by a disgusting hangover. *Oh, you're isolating yourself from your emotions because they're literally too much for you to handle? OK, you can do that for a bit . . . all right, that's enough. WELCOME BACK TO REALITY, BITCH! GET BACK TO YOUR SUFFERING!!!*

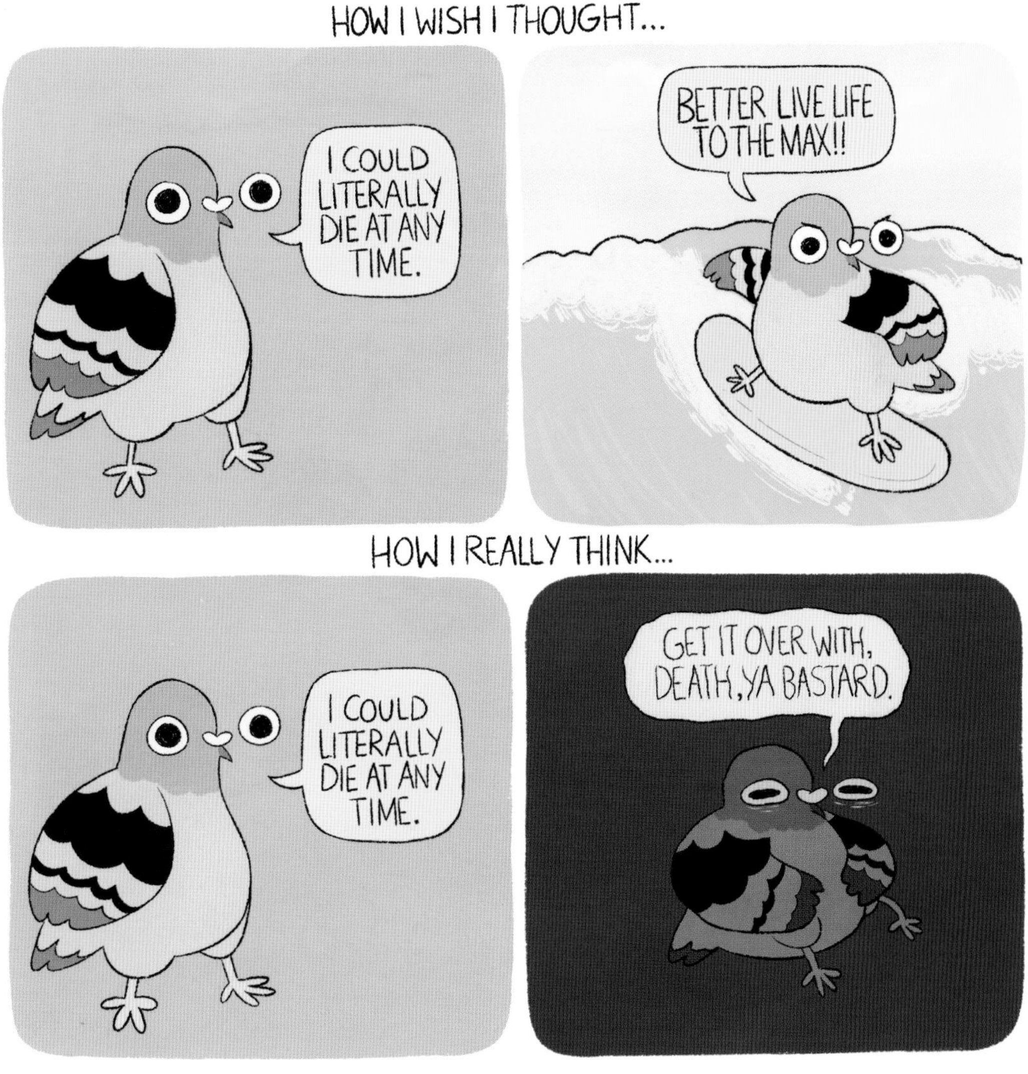
HOW I WISH I THOUGHT...
I COULD LITERALLY DIE AT ANY TIME.
BETTER LIVE LIFE TO THE MAX!!
HOW I REALLY THINK...
I COULD LITERALLY DIE AT ANY TIME.
GET IT OVER WITH, DEATH, YA BASTARD.

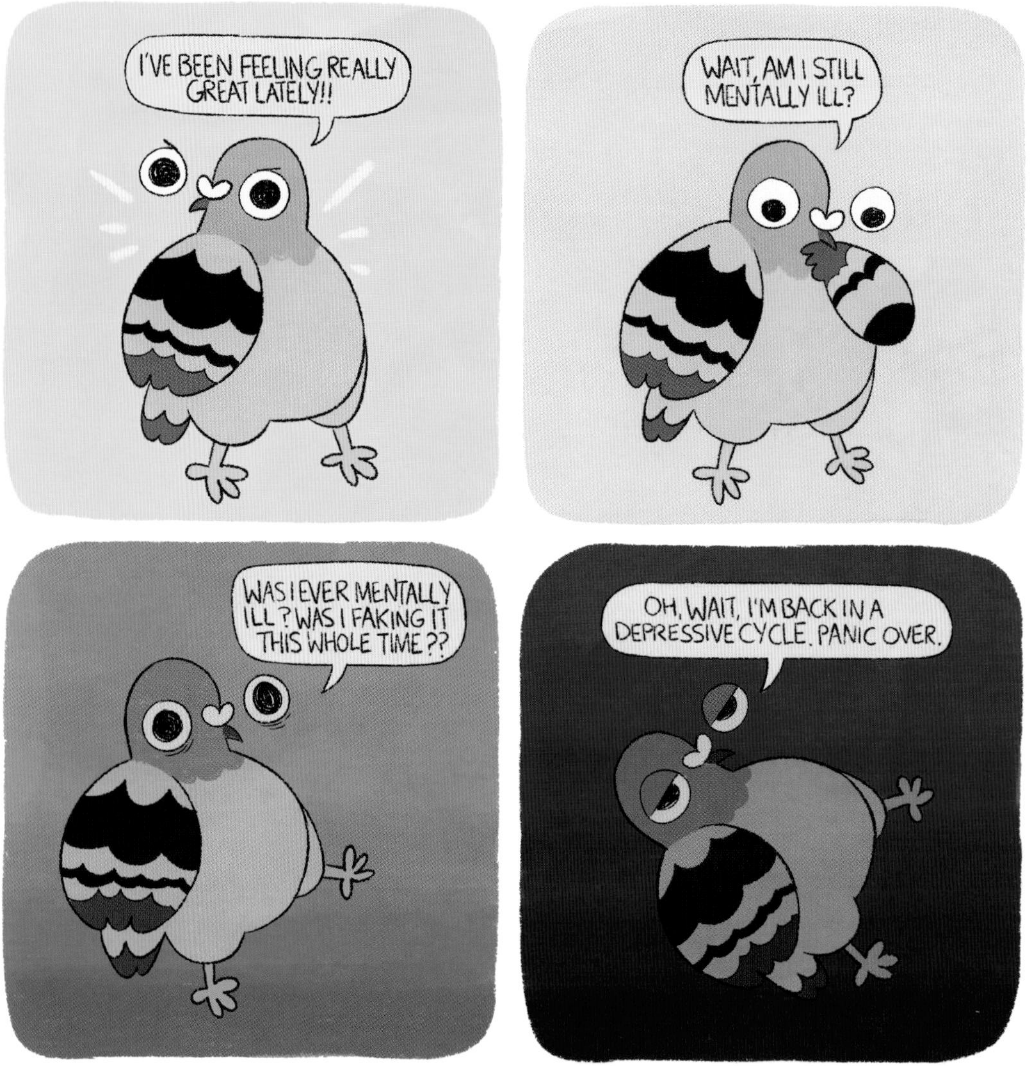

I'VE BEEN FEELING REALLY GREAT LATELY!!
WAIT, AM I STILL MENTALLY ILL?
WAS I EVER MENTALLY ILL? WAS I FAKING IT THIS WHOLE TIME??
OH, WAIT, I'M BACK IN A DEPRESSIVE CYCLE. PANIC OVER.

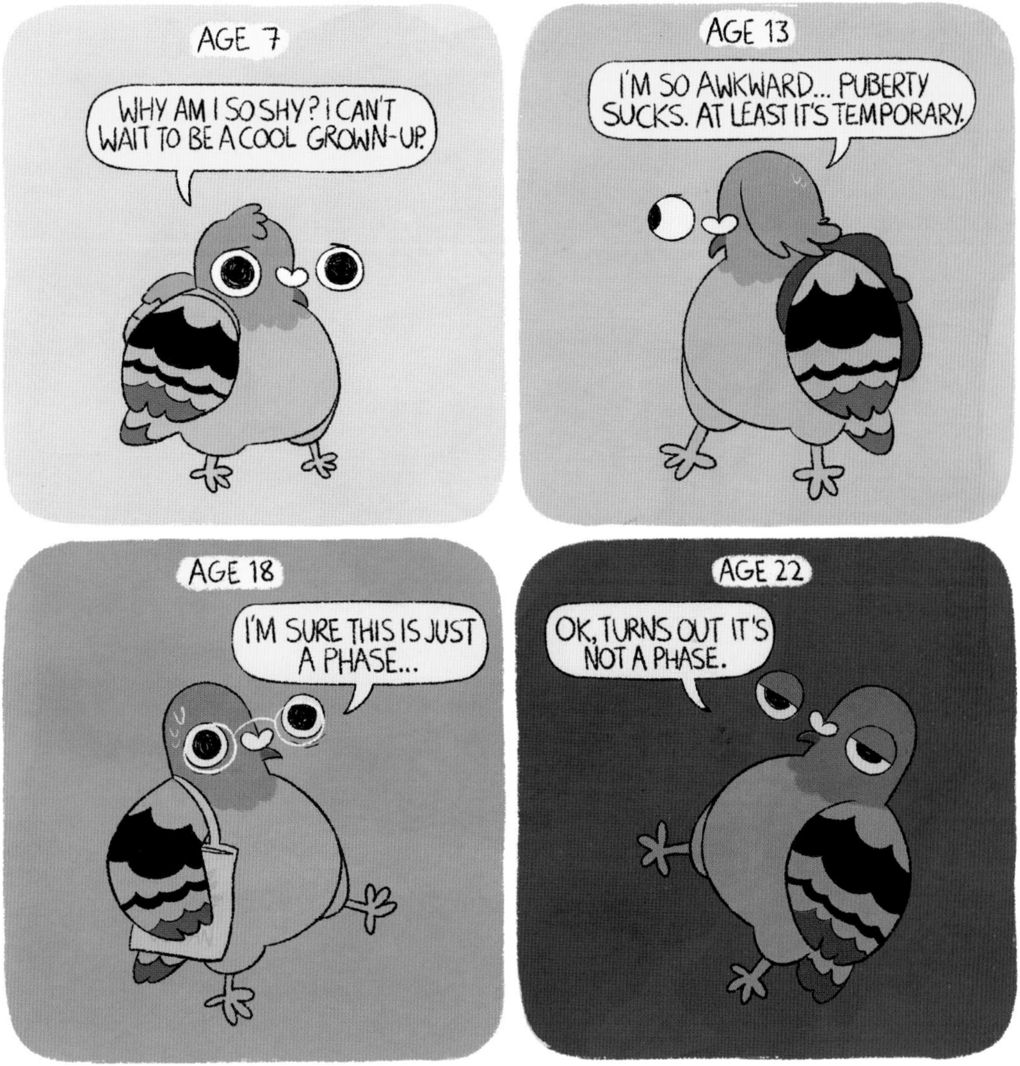
AGE 7
WHY AM I SO SHY? I CAN'T WAIT TO BE A COOL GROWN-UP.
AGE 13
I'M SO AWKWARD... PUBERTY SUCKS. AT LEAST IT'S TEMPORARY.
AGE 18
I'M SURE THIS IS JUST A PHASE...
AGE 22
OK, TURNS OUT IT'S NOT A PHASE.

ALL YOU CAN DO IS YOUR BEST...
AND SOMETIMES YOUR BEST IS
JUST EATING A SHIT TON OF ICE CREAM
WHILE GAZING INTO SPACE.

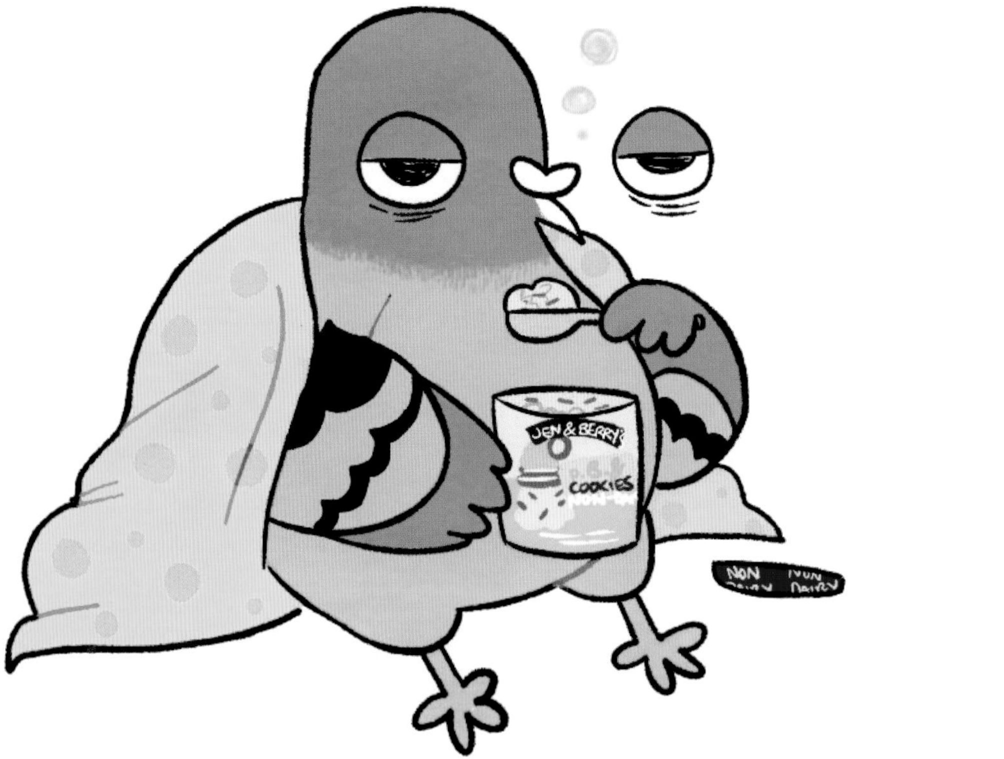

JEN & BERRY'S
COOKIES
NON

RELATIONSHIPS

Back in the introduction to "Bad Times" I mentioned how I was completely caught off-guard by the intense emotional onslaught that mental illness can bring. In the same vein, I was immensely underprepared for just how much depression and anxiety would impact my relationships with others. I promise I'm not as much of an oblivious dumbass as these things might make me seem. One of the biggest problems of mental illness is that it can make you so self-absorbed. Not in a narcissistic way, but in the sense that you're so hyper-focused on scrutinizing every aspect of yourself, you can forget to pay attention to your relationships with others. You spend so long watering one flower to death that another dies from dehydration.

Keeping in contact with people requires an active effort, and sometimes it is almost impossible to find the will to do anything when you're grappling with mental illness. I'm not saying that mentally ill people should have a free pass to ignore everyone around them and yet have their relationships stay the same.

I'm just saying it can be harder to keep nurturing relationships when you're depressed. Maintaining friendships is tough when all you want to do is hole yourself up in bed and fester in your own self-hatred. *Sorry, Erica, I can't come to your birthday drinks. I'll be busy fusing with the sofa during a daylong dissociative episode.*

Making the physical effort to touch base with the outside world when you're a shell of a person is difficult as it is. When you throw in all the anxious, paranoid thoughts that mental illness inspires, it becomes a lot more of an ordeal. Is this person mad at me for taking awhile to respond to their text? Was I boring? Do they hate me now? Why would they even like me in the first place? I don't deserve love or basic human kindness. Why should I even bother? I should just go and live in a cave by the sea for the rest of my life. Hopefully, the fish will tolerate me.

Trying to explain to people all the complex emotions and mental gymnastics that have been forced upon me has been hard. Really hard. It took a long time for *me* to recognize what I was going through; sharing the horrors with those I love, desperately hoping that they would understand—or at least want to try to understand—was unbelievably petrifying. I felt like both the frog on the dissecting table and the hand slicing it open. There are still parts of me and my experiences that I can't bring myself to divulge, or even dwell upon for too long, but carving up the areas I have shared has exposed much more than I ever thought possible—and I don't really regret it.

What I have disclosed has been remarkably well received; I'm very lucky to have such open and forward-thinking people in my life. But opening up has not been a straightforward, linear process. Just because someone knows about my anxiety and depression, that doesn't mean my relationship with them will instantly be smooth sailing. Relationships, by their nature, all face challenges and have their ups and downs. The challenges in your relationships when you're mentally ill are just of a different kind: how you communicate is fundamentally different from how someone without mental illness communicates, and you have to learn to bridge that gap.

This hasn't even covered relating to people I don't care deeply for. Not everyone will get what's going on in my brain. There have been several instances when I've been around someone who has spouted ignorant bullshit about mental illness—people I've just met, or people I only kind of know—and I still have to go about interacting with them. Sometimes I try to educate these people on why they can't say the abhorrent word-vomit they've just puked up, but a lot of the time, I just can't be bothered. You can only try so hard to teach certain people before you realize they're not interested in learning, and you just have to ball up all your frustration and mentally punt it across the earth.

"Relationships" will explore all the notions that I've just briefly described. This section expresses some of my different experiences in trying to connect with others, and how I view myself in relation to them, while my mental illness continuously makes me slap my face with my own hand. They depict relationships of all kinds: the romantic, the platonic, and the I-kind-of-know-you-but-not-really-so-I-can't-call-you-out-on-this. Some are inspired by epiphanies I've had, coming to terms with how my relationships with others are unavoidably influenced by my disorders. A few even lift dialogues directly from real encounters I've had. It may be cowardly to respond to comments that happened months ago through comics rather than a mature, face-to-face chat, but whatever. Fuck you, Sharon. Read a book.

SOMETIMES, I GET SAD
FOR NO REASON,

AND I FEEL LIKE I'M
NOT REALLY HERE,

BUT MY LOVED ONES GIVE ME THE
STRENGTH TO GET THROUGH IT...

AND THE HOPE THAT TOMORROW
WILL BE BETTER.

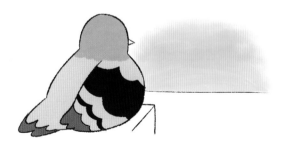

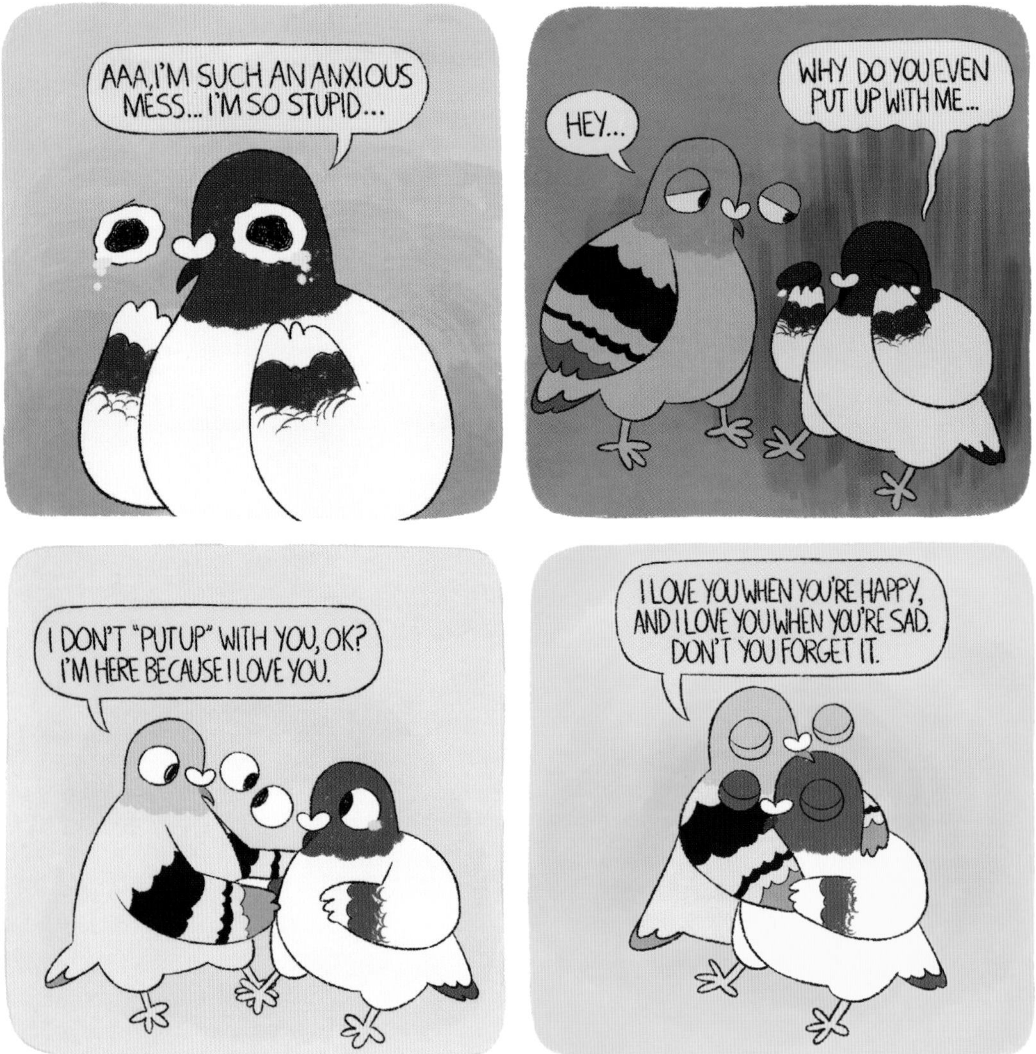
AAA, I'M SUCH AN ANXIOUS MESS... I'M SO STUPID...
HEY...
WHY DO YOU EVEN PUT UP WITH ME...
I DON'T "PUT UP" WITH YOU, OK? I'M HERE BECAUSE I LOVE YOU.
I LOVE YOU WHEN YOU'RE HAPPY, AND I LOVE YOU WHEN YOU'RE SAD. DON'T YOU FORGET IT.

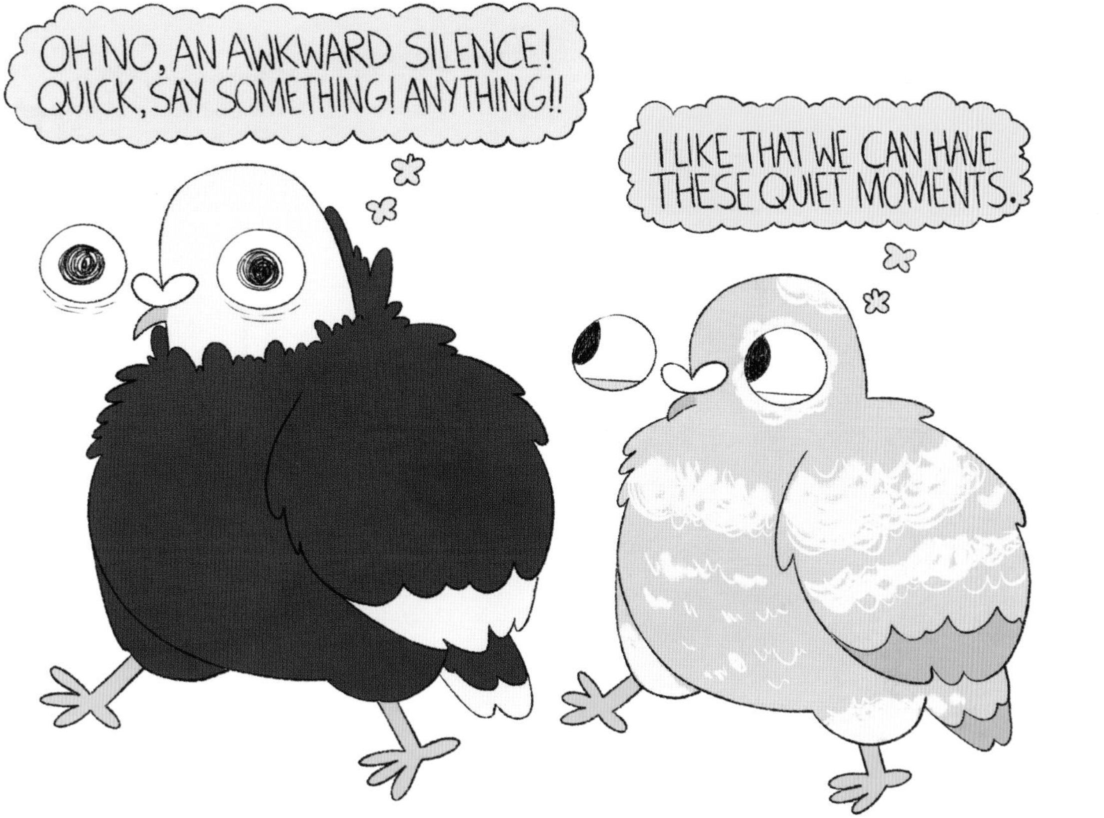
OH NO, AN AWKWARD SILENCE! QUICK, SAY SOMETHING! ANYTHING!!
I LIKE THAT WE CAN HAVE THESE QUIET MOMENTS.

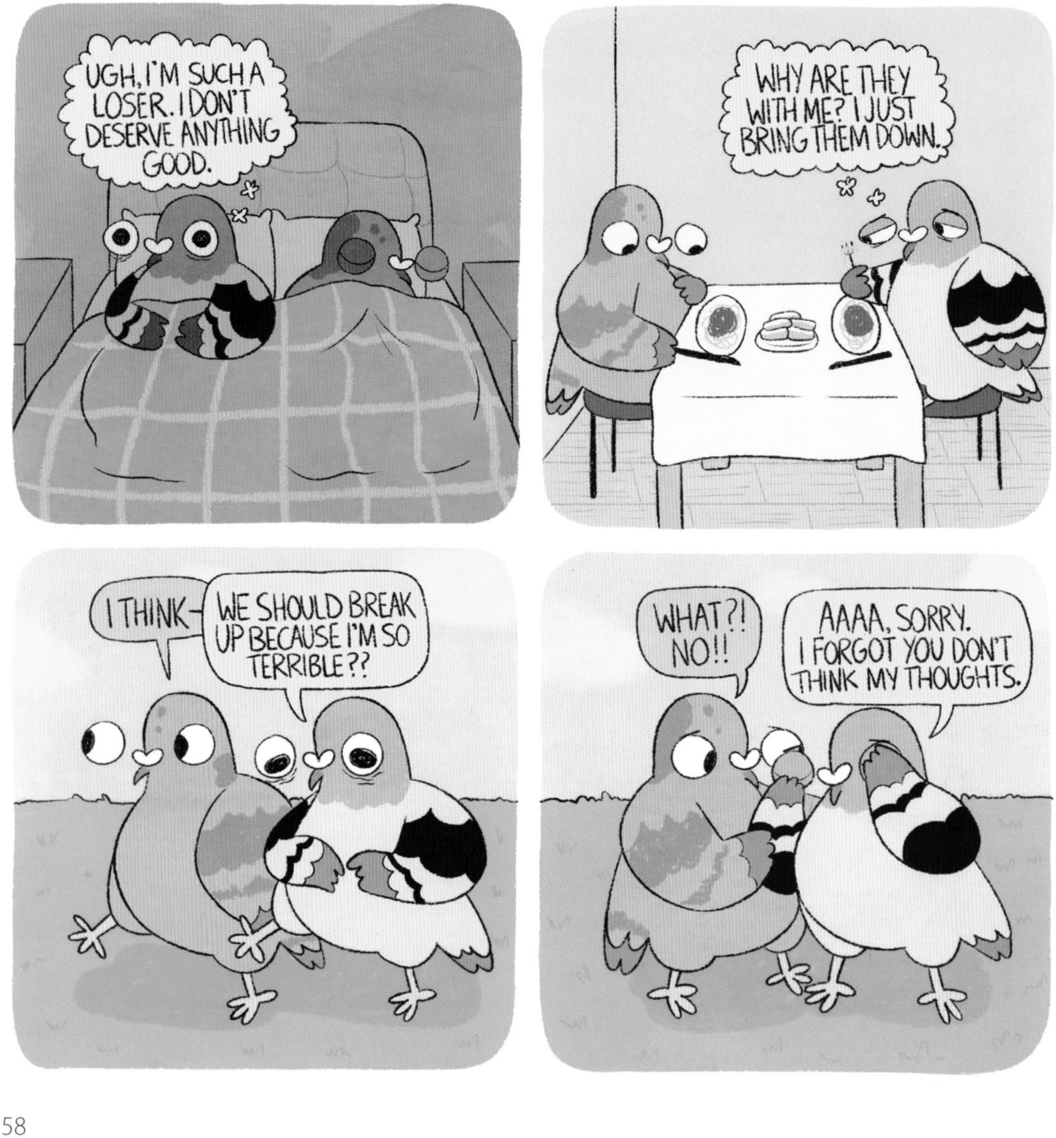
UGH, I'M SUCH A LOSER. I DON'T DESERVE ANYTHING GOOD.
WHY ARE THEY WITH ME? I JUST BRING THEM DOWN.
I THINK-
WE SHOULD BREAK UP BECAUSE I'M SO TERRIBLE??
WHAT?! NO!!
AAAA, SORRY. I FORGOT YOU DON'T THINK MY THOUGHTS.

I LOVE YOU.
I LOVE YOU, TOO!
I HOPE SHE DOESN'T THINK I SAY THAT TOO MUCH.
I'LL NEVER GET TIRED OF HEARING THAT!

I could barely manage to tolerate my own bullshit on good days; the thought of finding someone else willing to put up with me was laughable. Everyone feels a certain degree of awe that their partner chose them, of all the people in the world, but in my case, it felt extreme. My brain continuously reminded me of how ugly and boring I was. I was too much hassle and incapable of doing anything right. Even if by some miracle I did find someone who liked me, keeping up a healthy relationship with them seemed completely unmanageable.

This kind of negative thinking is no longer nearly as prevalent in my mind as it used to be, which wouldn't have been possible if I didn't start telling myself that I *do* deserve love, and that I need to embrace it when it's offered. Sometimes, I still feel like I tricked my partner in some way. *Oh, you thought you were dating a functional human being? THINK AGAIN! It's too late to escape now!!* But the more I thought about it, the more I disagreed with the notion that you have to love yourself before anyone else will, or that you can't truly love somebody unless you love yourself. Love and support from others are crucial to getting better, and they're things that everyone deserves, despite whatever their stupid mind says.

I'd be lying if I said my mental illnesses don't impact my relationships, and it's hard on both me and my partner to cope with them sometimes. But look, relationships are hard work regardless of whether you've got funky brain issues or not. They require a lot of effort and upkeep, and you can do everything perfectly by the book but still have rough patches. I just try to view my mental health as something like having a different work schedule than your partner; it's not something you can necessarily control, but you've both got to put in the time to make things work despite it.

True, you can't rely solely on the validation of others to improve your mental state, but it's pretty reassuring to have someone who wants to be with you, who isn't repulsed by your baggage. There's also no shame in requiring a little hyping-up or comfort from your partner every now and then. Praise is delicious. Feed me compliments until I'm like a fat cat basking in the sunlight. I deserve to have love thrown at me! And so do you! You're amazing!

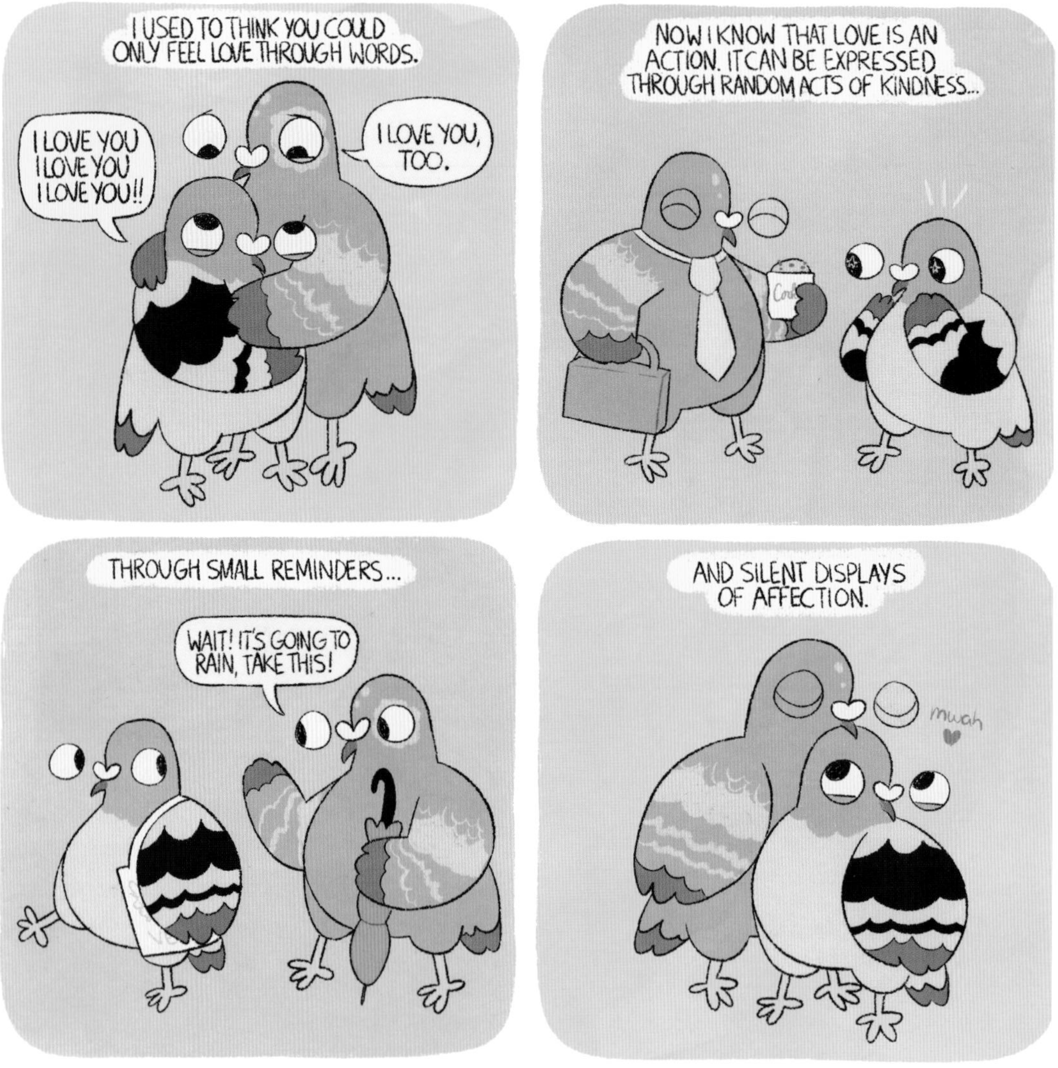
I USED TO THINK YOU COULD ONLY FEEL LOVE THROUGH WORDS.
I LOVE YOU I LOVE YOU I LOVE YOU!!
I LOVE YOU, TOO.
NOW I KNOW THAT LOVE IS AN ACTION. IT CAN BE EXPRESSED THROUGH RANDOM ACTS OF KINDNESS...
THROUGH SMALL REMINDERS...
WAIT! IT'S GOING TO RAIN, TAKE THIS!
AND SILENT DISPLAYS OF AFFECTION.
mwah

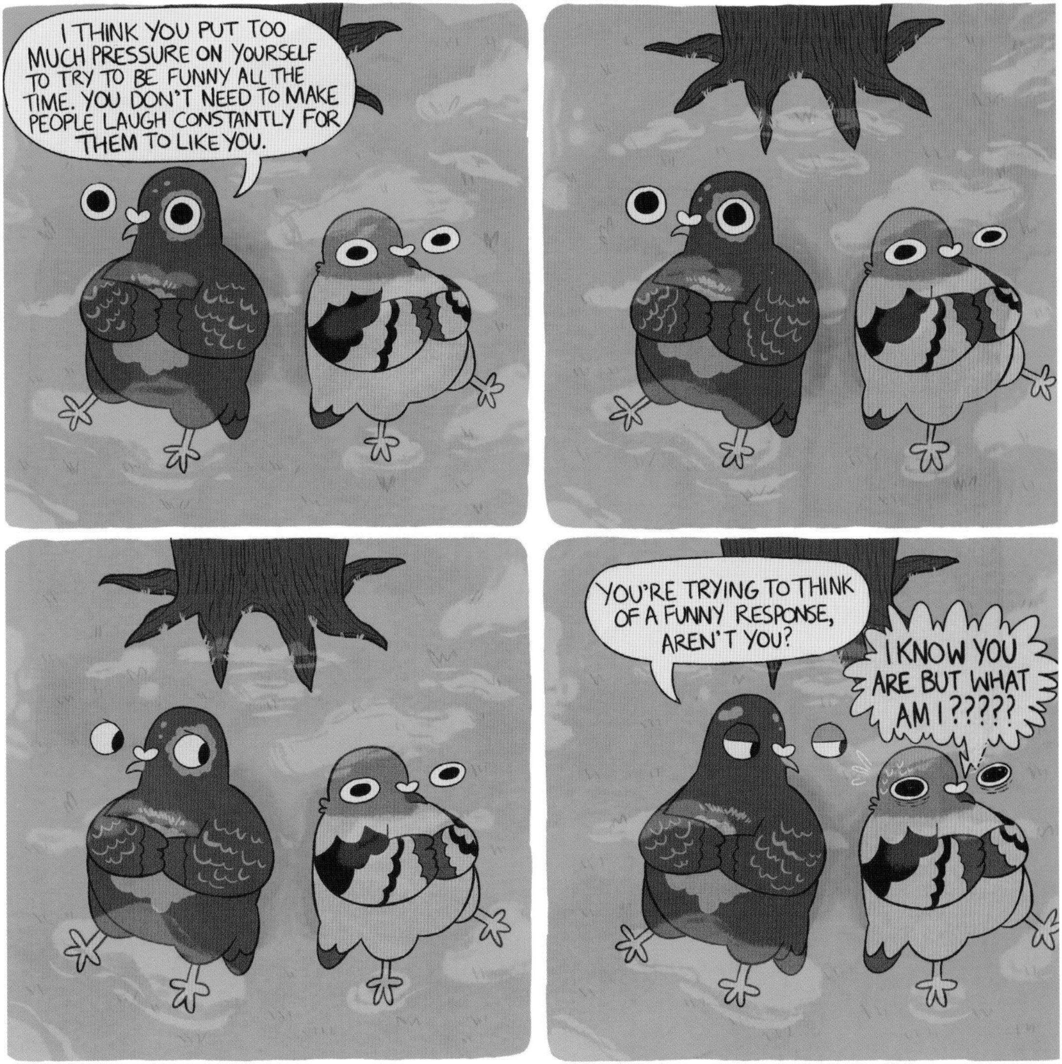
I THINK YOU PUT TOO MUCH PRESSURE ON YOURSELF TO TRY TO BE FUNNY ALL THE TIME. YOU DON'T NEED TO MAKE PEOPLE LAUGH CONSTANTLY FOR THEM TO LIKE YOU.
YOU'RE TRYING TO THINK OF A FUNNY RESPONSE, AREN'T YOU?
I KNOW YOU ARE BUT WHAT AM I?????

YOUR FLAWS

- SNORES
- GRUMPY IN THE MORNING
- ??? THAT'S IT PRETTY MUCH

MY FLAWS

- NEEDY
- TOO SENSITIVE
- CRIES A LOT FOR NO REASON
- BASICALLY TRASH
- WHY ARE YOU WITH ME???

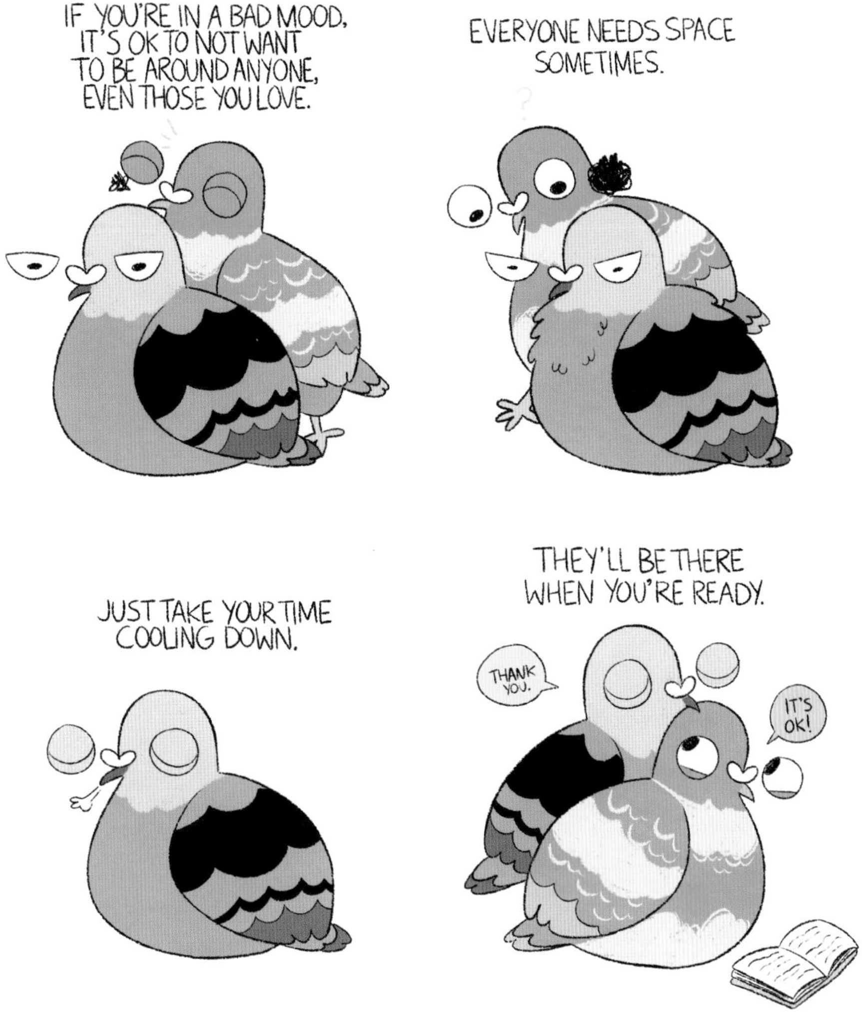
IF YOU'RE IN A BAD MOOD, IT'S OK TO NOT WANT TO BE AROUND ANYONE, EVEN THOSE YOU LOVE.
EVERYONE NEEDS SPACE SOMETIMES.
JUST TAKE YOUR TIME COOLING DOWN.
THEY'LL BE THERE WHEN YOU'RE READY.
THANK YOU.
IT'S OK!

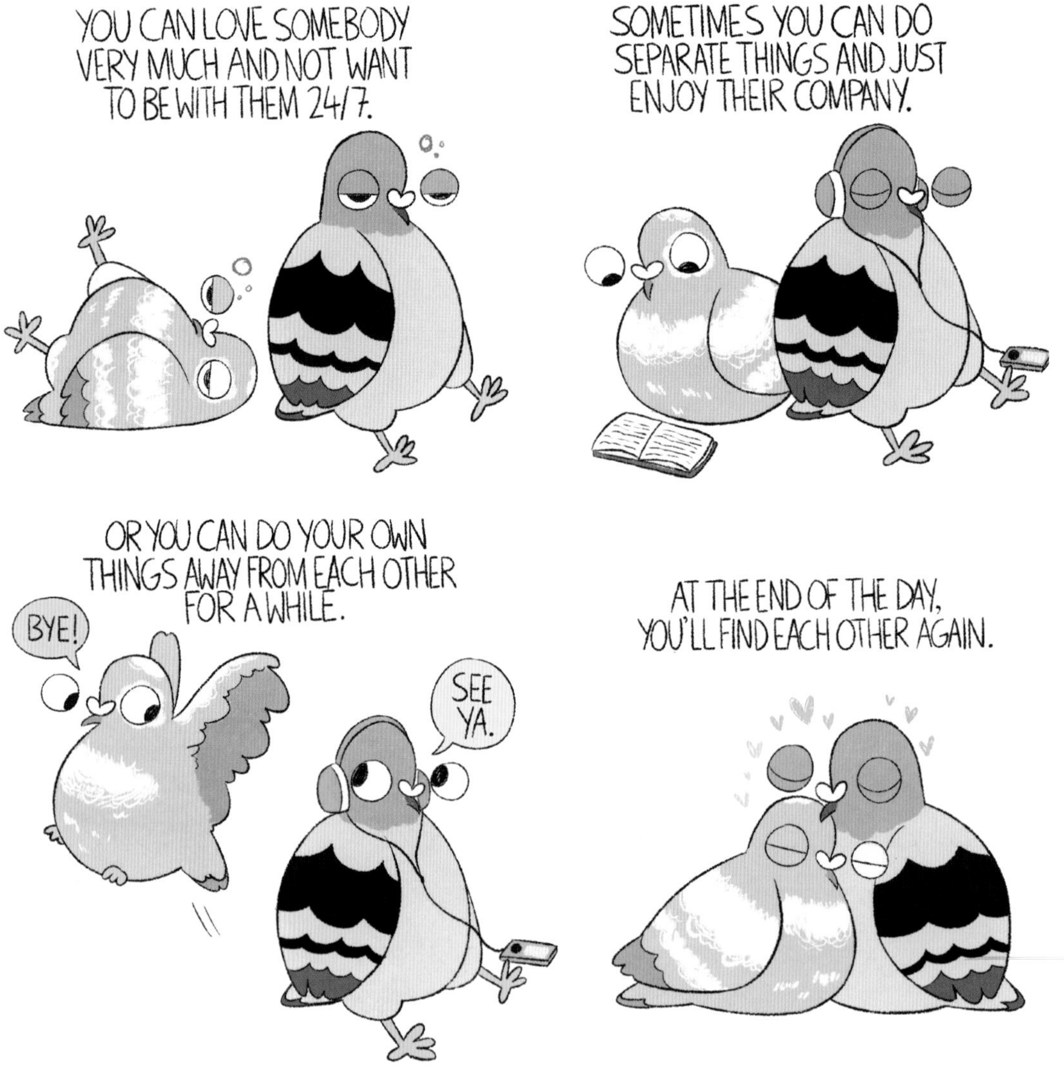
YOU CAN LOVE SOMEBODY VERY MUCH AND NOT WANT TO BE WITH THEM 24/7.
SOMETIMES YOU CAN DO SEPARATE THINGS AND JUST ENJOY THEIR COMPANY.
OR YOU CAN DO YOUR OWN THINGS AWAY FROM EACH OTHER FOR A WHILE.
BYE!
SEE YA.
AT THE END OF THE DAY, YOU'LL FIND EACH OTHER AGAIN.

I've always been a little over-affectionate, but when my anxiety was at its worst, I felt like I became the neediest person on the planet. It was as if there was something wriggling inside of me with a voracious appetite for approval that was never satisfied. Sort of like an emotional tapeworm. I'd constantly need to be told, "I love you" or "You're not bothering me." If I detected even the slightest amount of annoyance, real or imaginary, a wave of guilt and self-loathing would crash over me. It would ebb away at any belief that I deserved love in the first place. *You fool! You ARE bothering them! You're asking the same question over and over again! That IS annoying!!! But keep doing it.*

I've never fully trusted my brain's analysis of other people's demeanors, because it would usually just boil down to, "Uhh, idk they hate you." I had to forcefully remind myself that people can sound annoyed for a variety of reasons: they had a shit day at work, or they're tired, or they have a lot of personal stuff going on, or maybe they just woke up in a bad mood for absolutely no reason because the human spectrum of emotion is vast and sometimes cannot be explained in any rational way. Whatever the reason, I shouldn't take it so personally because, sadly, the world does not revolve around me.

On the flip side, if I wanted some alone time, then I really did not want to be bothered at all. I was only one step away from hissing at people who invaded my personal space during these moments. Again, it's taken some effort to cope with this in a healthy manner. I felt ashamed of my need for personal space, because it seemed a lot more frequent than the norm. But needing space is absolutely normal and, in my view, is in fact crucial every now and then, but I had to stop myself from being a complete dick about it. It's totally fine to say, "I need some time to myself right now, thanks for understanding" to someone instead of growling at them from under a blanket fort.

All in all, it's taken me a long time to understand that it's OK to need expressions of validation and love, and it's also OK to be by yourself for a bit, even if these needs seem a little excessive at times. They can both be embraced in a totally healthy manner. I know this seems quite remedial, but it was a big step for me, all right?

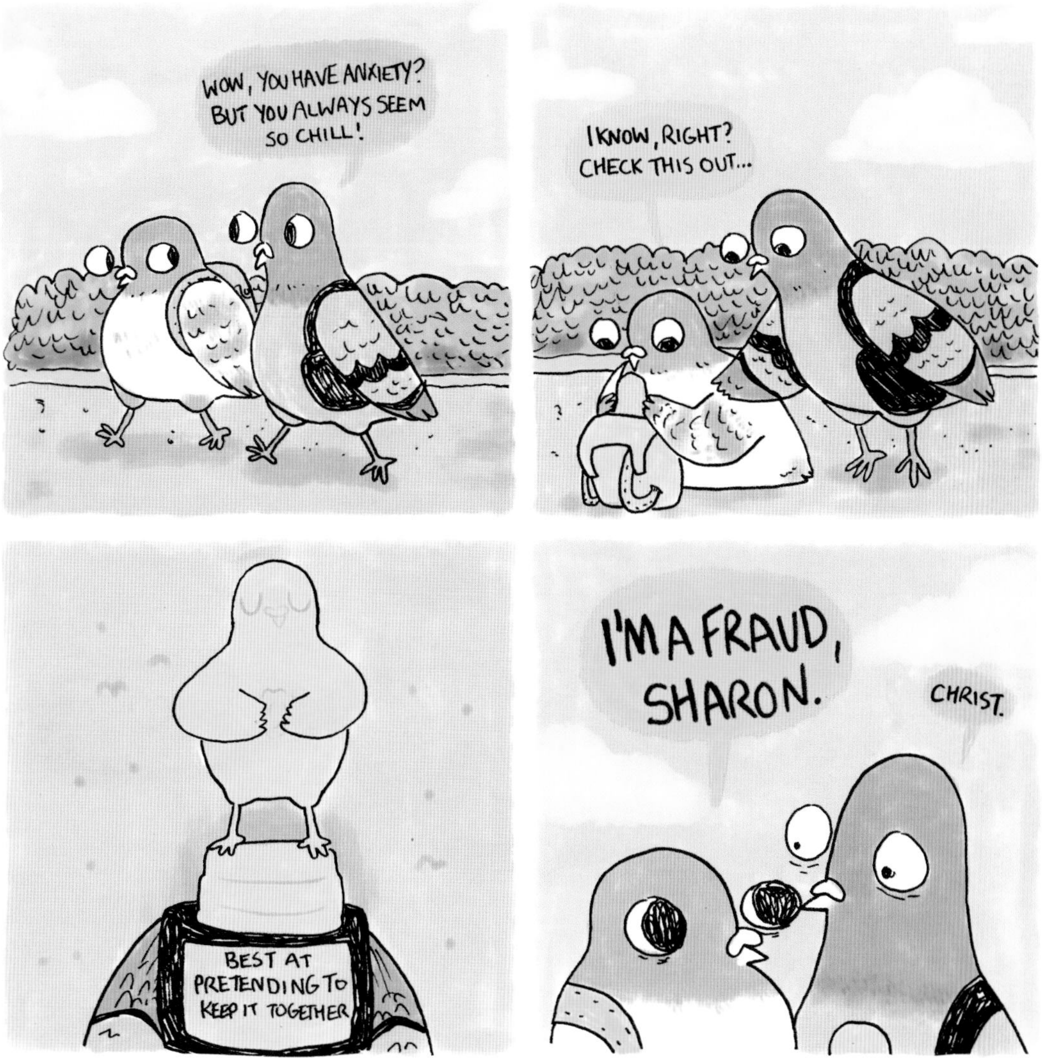
WOW, YOU HAVE ANXIETY? BUT YOU ALWAYS SEEM SO CHILL!
I KNOW, RIGHT? CHECK THIS OUT...
BEST AT PRETENDING TO KEEP IT TOGETHER
I'M A FRAUD, SHARON.
CHRIST.

YOU'RE SO QUIET!
IMPULSE
I HAVE ANXIETY SHARON
REALITY
HAHA... YEAH...

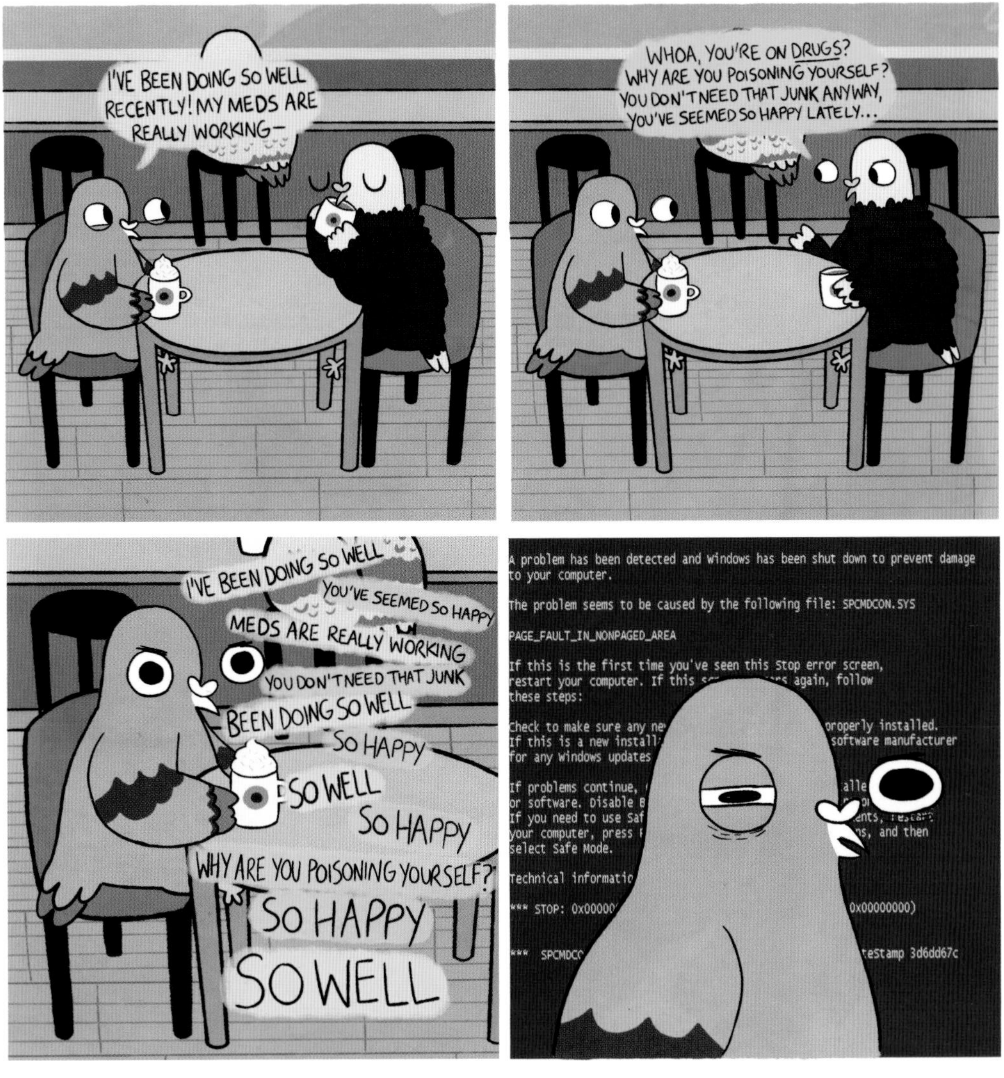
I'VE BEEN DOING SO WELL RECENTLY! MY MEDS ARE REALLY WORKING—
WHOA, YOU'RE ON DRUGS? WHY ARE YOU POISONING YOURSELF? YOU DON'T NEED THAT JUNK ANYWAY, YOU'VE SEEMED SO HAPPY LATELY...
I'VE BEEN DOING SO WELL
YOU'VE SEEMED SO HAPPY
MEDS ARE REALLY WORKING
YOU DON'T NEED THAT JUNK
BEEN DOING SO WELL
SO HAPPY
SO WELL
SO HAPPY
WHY ARE YOU POISONING YOURSELF?
SO HAPPY
SO WELL
A problem has been detected and windows has been shut down to prevent damage
to your computer.
The problem seems to be caused by the following file: SPCMDCON.SYS
PAGE_FAULT_IN_NONPAGED_AREA
If this is the first time you've seen this Stop error screen,
restart your computer. If this
again, follow
these steps:
Check to make sure any ne
properly installed.
If this is a new install
software manufacturer
for any windows updates
If problems continue,
or software. Disable B
If you need to use Saf
your computer, press F
ns, and then
select Safe Mode.
Technical informatio
*** STOP: 0x0000
0x00000000)
*** SPCMDC
teStamp 3d6dd67c

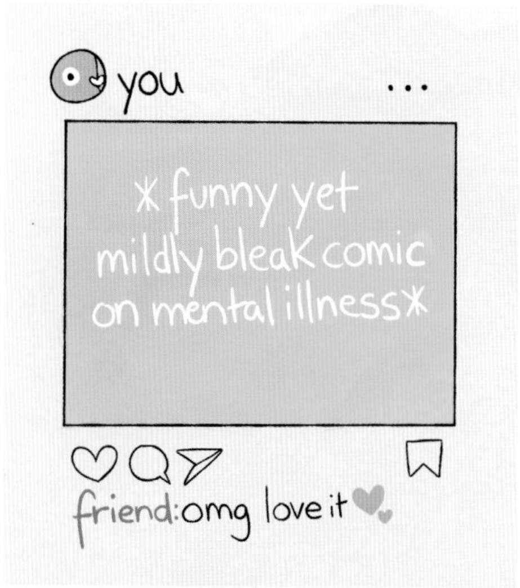
you
funny yet mildly bleak comic on mental illness
friend: omg love it

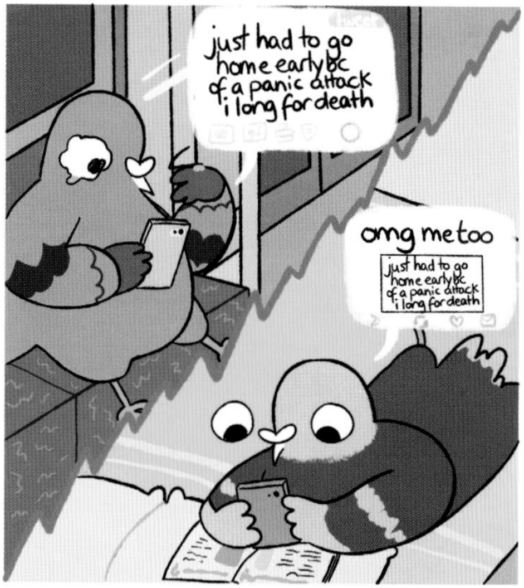
just had to go home early bc of a panic attack i long for death
omg me too
just had to go home early bc of a panic attack i long for death

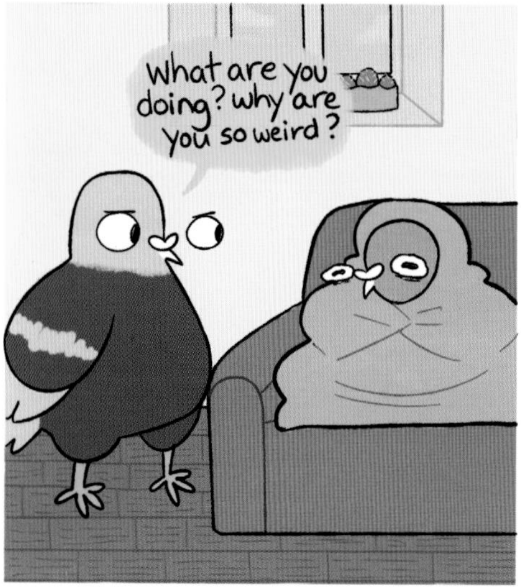
What are you doing? why are you so weird?

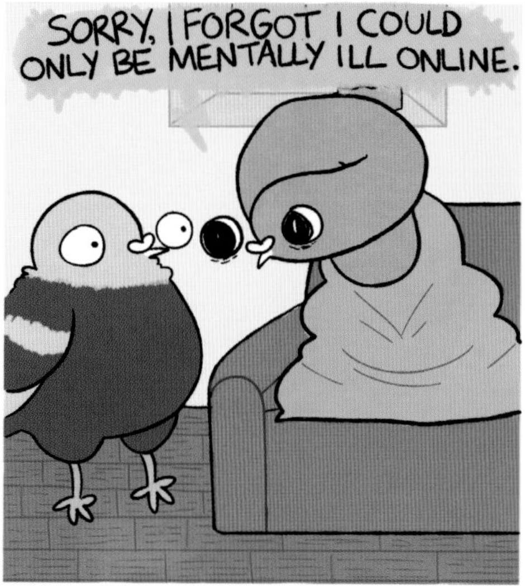
SORRY, I FORGOT I COULD ONLY BE MENTALLY ILL ONLINE.

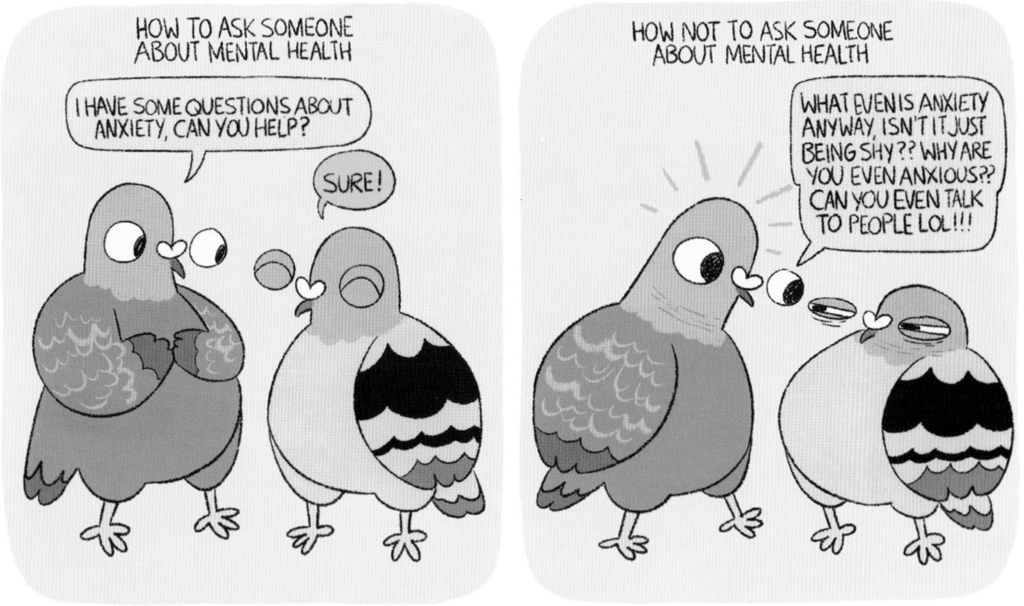
HOW TO ASK SOMEONE ABOUT MENTAL HEALTH
I HAVE SOME QUESTIONS ABOUT ANXIETY, CAN YOU HELP?
SURE!
HOW NOT TO ASK SOMEONE ABOUT MENTAL HEALTH
WHAT EVEN IS ANXIETY ANYWAY, ISN'T IT JUST BEING SHY?? WHY ARE YOU EVEN ANXIOUS?? CAN YOU EVEN TALK TO PEOPLE LOL!!!

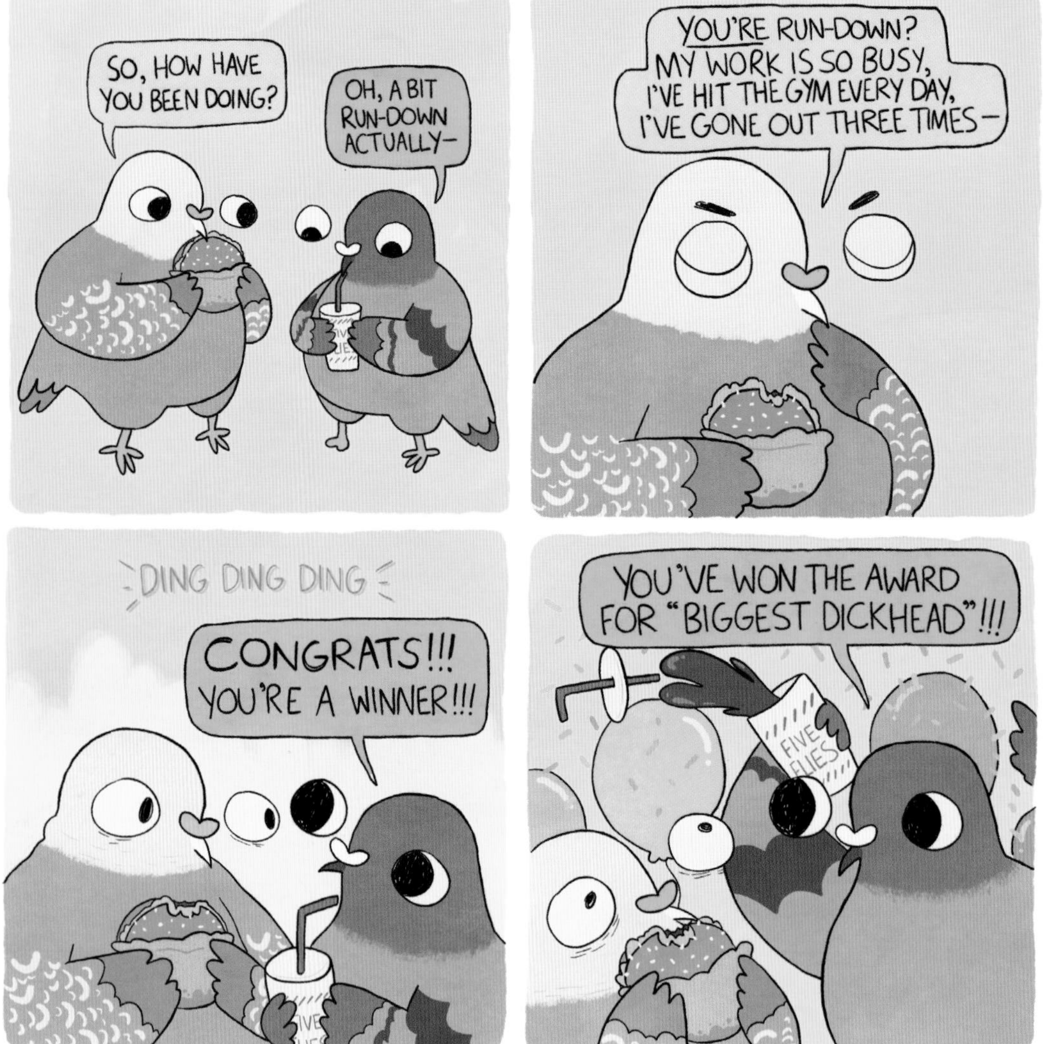
SO, HOW HAVE YOU BEEN DOING?
OH, A BIT RUN-DOWN ACTUALLY–
YOU'RE RUN-DOWN? MY WORK IS SO BUSY, I'VE HIT THE GYM EVERY DAY, I'VE GONE OUT THREE TIMES–
DING DING DING
CONGRATS!!! YOU'RE A WINNER!!!
YOU'VE WON THE AWARD FOR "BIGGEST DICKHEAD"!!!
FIVE FLIES

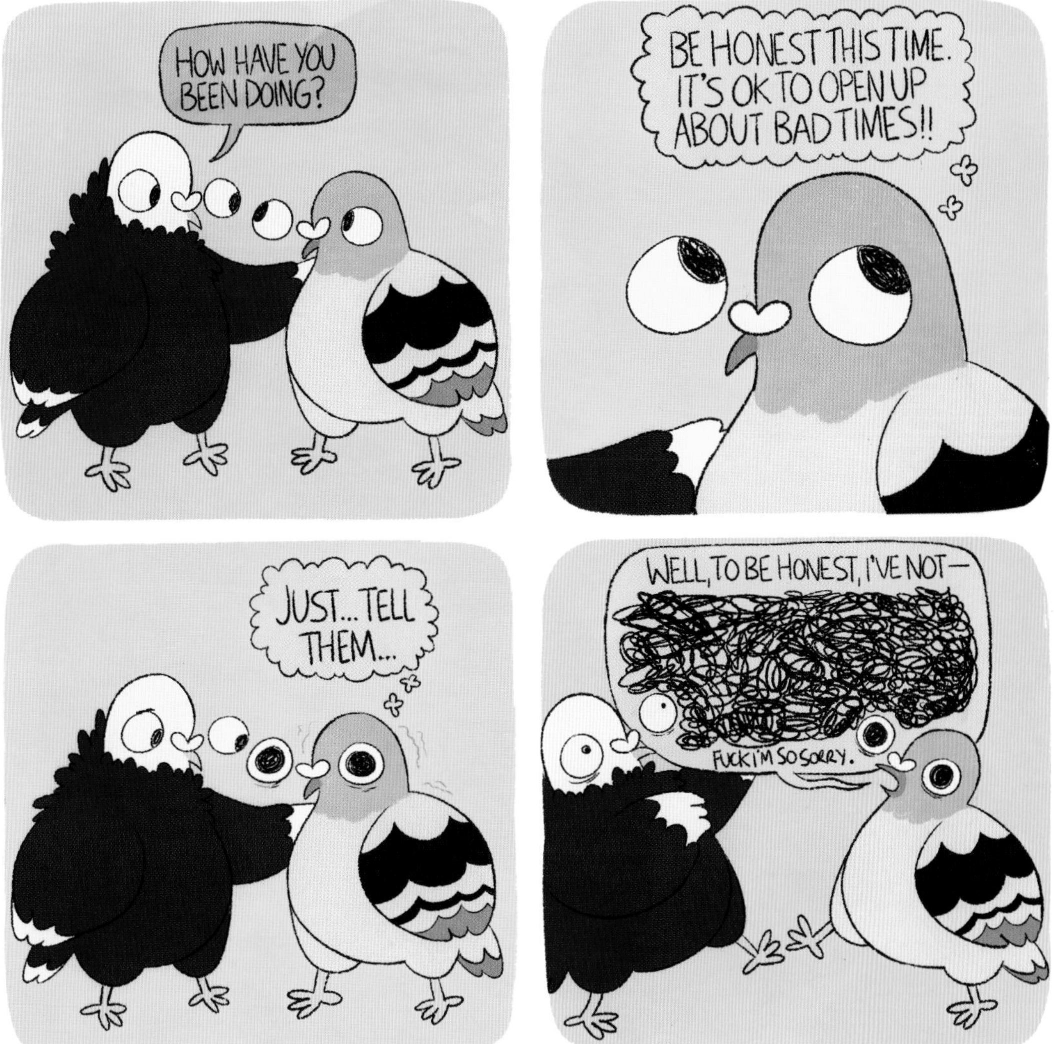
HOW HAVE YOU BEEN DOING?
BE HONEST THIS TIME. IT'S OK TO OPEN UP ABOUT BAD TIMES!!
JUST... TELL THEM...
WELL, TO BE HONEST, I'VE NOT—
FUCK I'M SO SORRY.

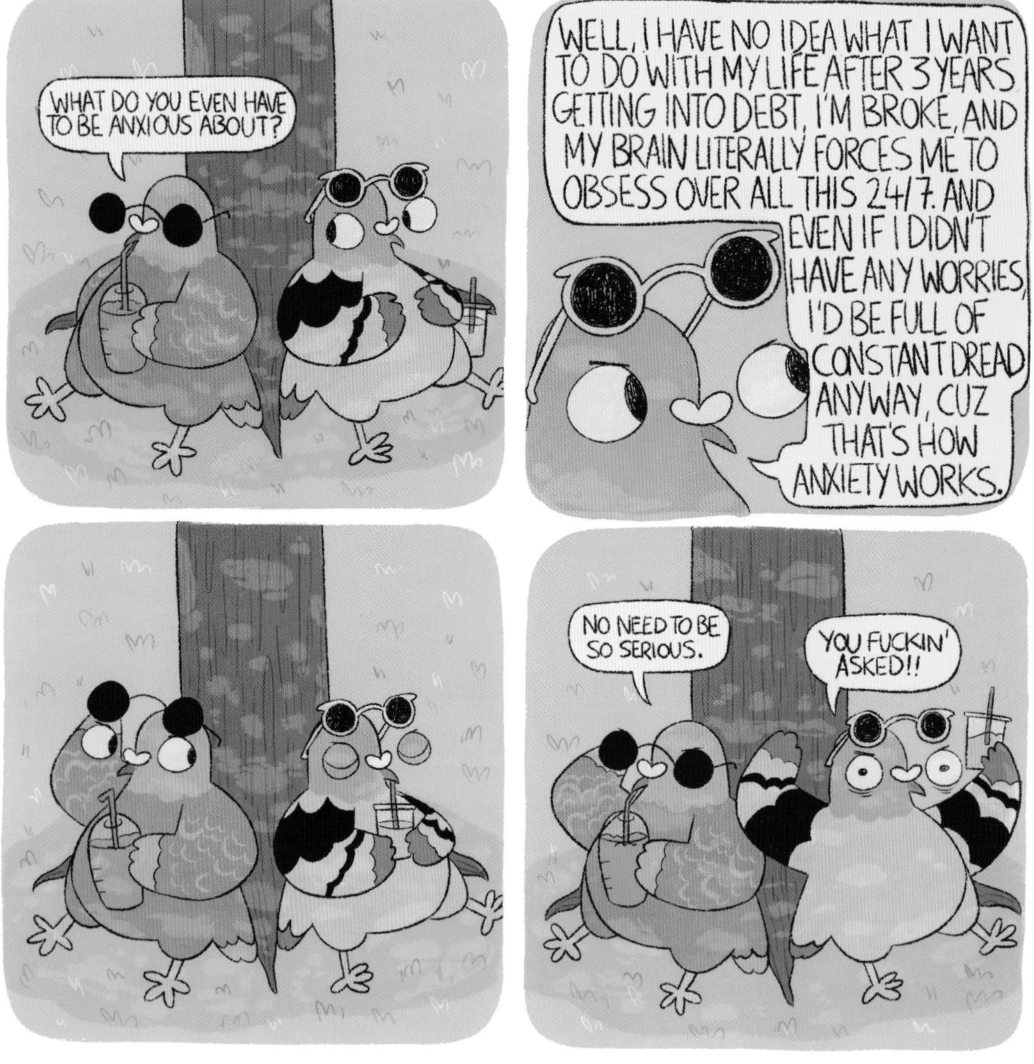
WHAT DO YOU EVEN HAVE TO BE ANXIOUS ABOUT?
WELL, I HAVE NO IDEA WHAT I WANT TO DO WITH MY LIFE AFTER 3 YEARS GETTING INTO DEBT, I'M BROKE, AND MY BRAIN LITERALLY FORCES ME TO OBSESS OVER ALL THIS 24/7. AND EVEN IF I DIDN'T HAVE ANY WORRIES, I'D BE FULL OF CONSTANT DREAD ANYWAY, CUZ THAT'S HOW ANXIETY WORKS.
NO NEED TO BE SO SERIOUS.
YOU FUCKIN' ASKED!!

I've been very lucky in the sense that all my loved ones have been unbelievably kind and supportive whenever my anxiety rears its big, gross head. They've been incredibly eager to learn about it, sometimes even undertaking research on anxiety on their own to gain a better understanding of what it's like to experience. I'm so, so grateful for them. Unfortunately, a good chunk of people in general have very little or no understanding at all of mental illness, which means I've received a lot of weird and idiotic questions about it.

No, anxiety doesn't mean I can't leave my house. No, depression doesn't mean I'm crying 24/7. No, it's not a phase. GOD, I wish it were, can you imagine?? I don't mind answering silly questions if they're coming from a place of sincere curiosity and the person honestly wants to understand things better, even if it makes me internally despair over the lack of mental health awareness in mainstream society. However, some people just seem to have their dickhead-o-meter cranked up to 101 all the time and genuinely cannot fathom the notion that some of the words they spew up might be a bit offensive.

"Anxiety? That's not an illness, everyone gets that." "Depression is all in your head. You have to force yourself to face the real world." "Mental illness is just a trend; you'll grow out of it." WOW, THANKS! I'M CURED! WHO WOULD'VE KNOWN I COULD MAKE ALL OF THAT GO AWAY BY JUST "NOT THINKING ABOUT IT"? THANK YOU SO MUCH, DOCTOR DICKHEAD,

FOR YOUR RADICAL NEW THERAPY OF INVALIDATING MY ENTIRE LIFE EXPERIENCE. HERE'S YOUR NOBEL PRIZE.

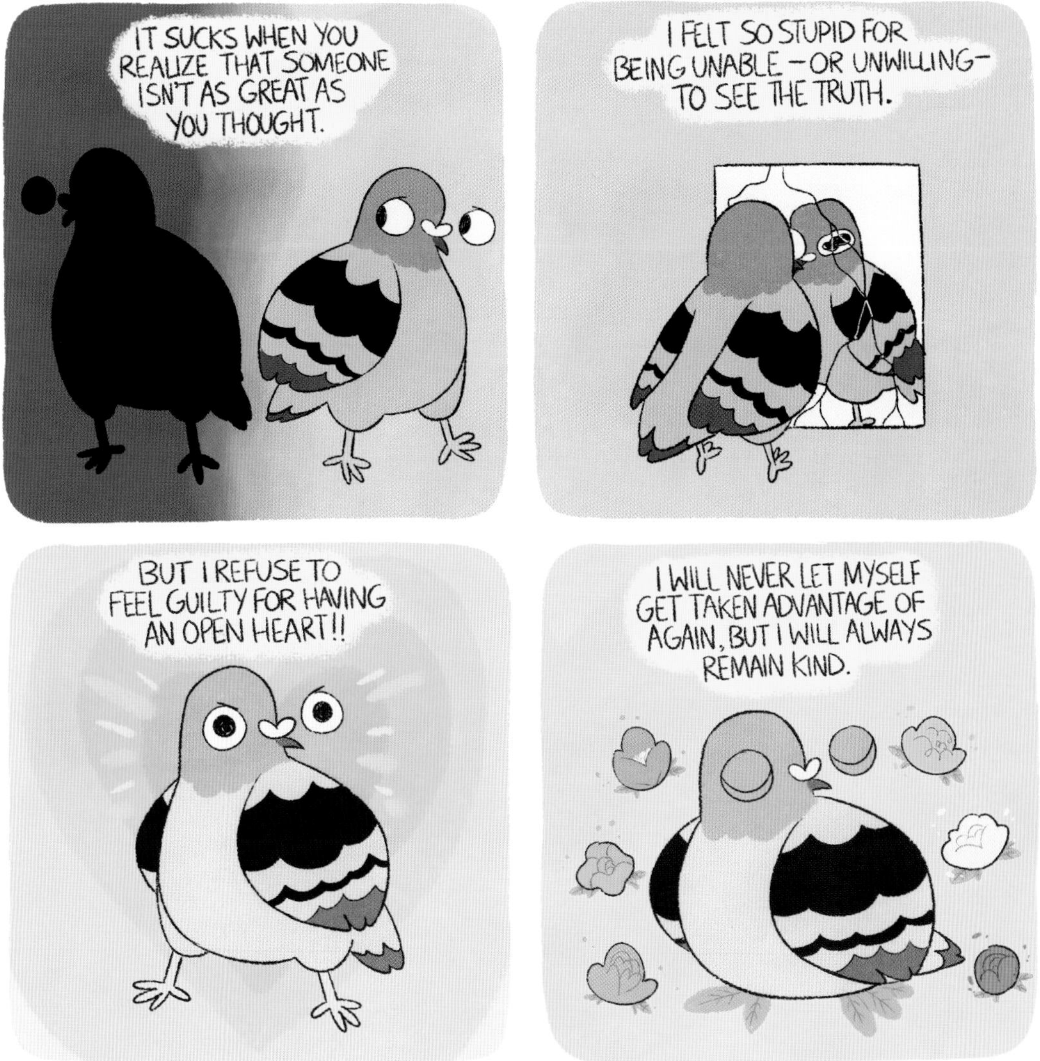
IT SUCKS WHEN YOU REALIZE THAT SOMEONE ISN'T AS GREAT AS YOU THOUGHT.
I FELT SO STUPID FOR BEING UNABLE — OR UNWILLING — TO SEE THE TRUTH.
BUT I REFUSE TO FEEL GUILTY FOR HAVING AN OPEN HEART!!
I WILL NEVER LET MYSELF GET TAKEN ADVANTAGE OF AGAIN, BUT I WILL ALWAYS REMAIN KIND.

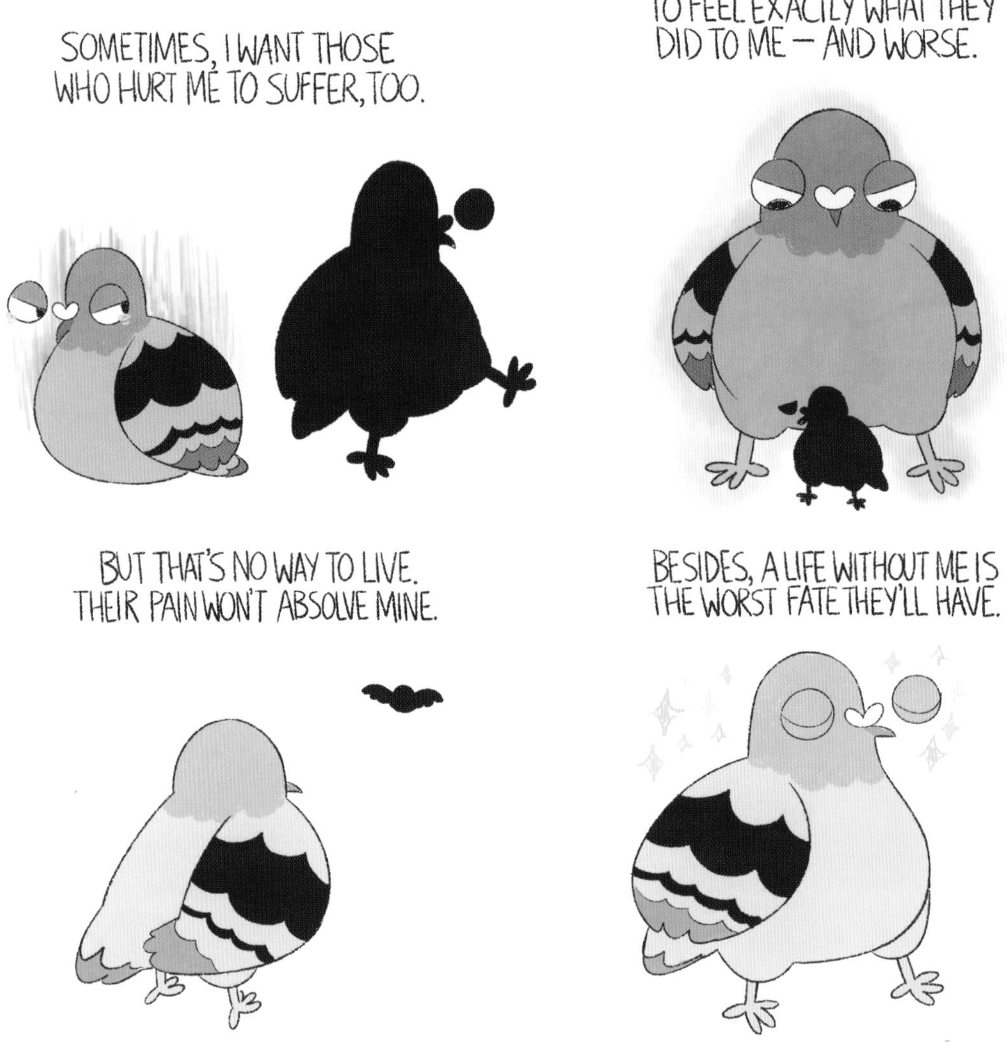
SOMETIMES, I WANT THOSE WHO HURT ME TO SUFFER, TOO.
TO FEEL EXACTLY WHAT THEY DID TO ME — AND WORSE.
BUT THAT'S NO WAY TO LIVE. THEIR PAIN WON'T ABSOLVE MINE.
BESIDES, A LIFE WITHOUT ME IS THE WORST FATE THEY'LL HAVE.

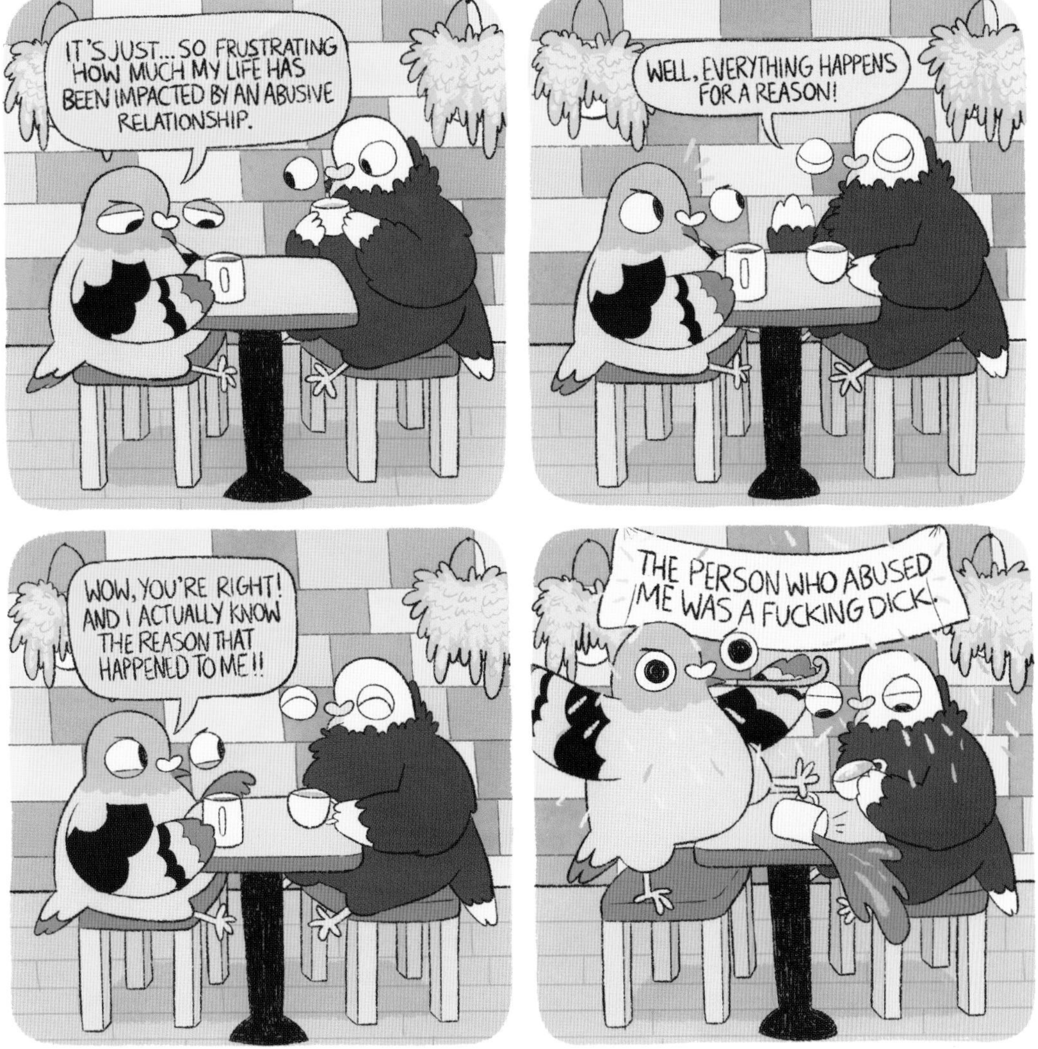
IT'S JUST... SO FRUSTRATING HOW MUCH MY LIFE HAS BEEN IMPACTED BY AN ABUSIVE RELATIONSHIP.
WELL, EVERYTHING HAPPENS FOR A REASON!
WOW, YOU'RE RIGHT! AND I ACTUALLY KNOW THE REASON THAT HAPPENED TO ME!!
THE PERSON WHO ABUSED ME WAS A FUCKING DICK.

I HAVE A RECURRING NIGHTMARE THAT I'M WITH YOU AGAIN.
YOU MAKE ME FEEL TOTALLY HELPLESS ALL OVER AGAIN.
YOU MAKE ME DO AWFUL THINGS THAT DRIVE AWAY THE ONES I LOVE.
BUT I ALWAYS WAKE UP EVENTUALLY, TO ANOTHER DAY THAT PUTS ME FARTHER AWAY FROM YOU.

The effects of emotional abuse are incredibly difficult to put into words. It's taken me about an hour to get beyond that sentence. How do you begin to describe the sensation of having your self-worth, your *sanity*, unrelentingly destroyed by somebody you love, who claims they love you back? Being in an abusive relationship was like having my anxiety and depression manifest in a physical person who validated every single negative thought I had about myself. It set my quest for self-improvement back further than I want to think about.

Just reflecting upon it makes my stomach churn. Every time I'd have my appearance joked about (read: insulted), or have my memory purposefully contradicted to suit their version of events, or be terrified of saying the wrong thing in case I tipped their mood, my entire body would become racked with white-hot shame and misery for hours. I think I always knew this person was terrible for me—terrible in general—but my sense of worth was so ground down I couldn't bring myself to leave. Being with them was a twisted form of self-abasement. I was already having such horrible thoughts about myself, and this person's treatment of me corroborated those feelings, so I felt relieved—I wasn't imagining things after all! I really *was* a worthless piece of dirt! Thanks for the support, babe!

I don't like thinking about it too much now. I spent a long time going through a dark period where the reality of what happened to me came abruptly crashing down, and I barely got through it. It sucks how much somebody can tear you down.

I'm pretty sure I would've made progress with my mental health a lot sooner if I didn't have a bunch of shitty relationship baggage to drag alongside me as well.

I don't think dealing with it has even made me a braver, better person; it's just made gaining an adequate sense of self-esteem more frustrating. There's nothing I can do about it now, though. I don't think I'll ever stop being angry about it, or affected by it in some way, but that's fine. I think I'm doing a good job of nurturing myself. I'm still growing, but small steps are better than none. I'm petty enough to admit that I take solace in the fact that I am an objectively better person than the one who hurt me. Suck on my theoretical good person points, ya prick.

I USED TO HAVE A BAD HABIT OF RELYING ON MY PARTNERS FOR MY SELF-ESTEEM.

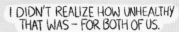

I DIDN'T REALIZE HOW UNHEALTHY THAT WAS – FOR BOTH OF US.

GIMMEE GIMMEE

WHEN THEY'D LEAVE, I'D FEEL SO, SO ALONE. I DIDN'T KNOW HOW TO LOVE MYSELF ON MY OWN.

BUT AFTER A LOT OF TIME AND PRACTICE, I THINK I'M PRETTY GOOD AT IT.

HOW I PROBABLY LOOK TALKING ABOUT MY ANXIETY
OH, Y'KNOW...IT'S UMM... WORRYING AND STUFF...
HOW I WORRY I LOOK
NNNNNNNNGGGGHHH
PLEASE PITY ME AND TREAT ME LIKE A TICKING BOMB I LOVE IT!!!!

SOMETIMES, I CAN'T HELP BUT
FEEL IN AWE OF OTHERS.

BUT MAYBE EVERYONE FEELS THAT WAY...
THEY JUST DON'T LET IT GET THEM DOWN.

As you may have guessed by now, my self-esteem isn't always the highest. I feel like everyone is more hypercritical of themselves than is necessary anyway, but anxiety amplifies any negative thought I have about myself and jumps to so many ridiculous conclusions it could qualify as an Olympic gymnast. My chin's a bit spotty today? I am a hideous monster, and if I go outside, everyone will shrivel away in disgust. I'm feeling a bit tired? Unacceptable. I am not allowed to feel tired. I must isolate myself to prevent this negative energy from spreading.

Over the years, however, I've become good at disguising any indication that I'm seconds away from a mental breakdown. A lot of people to whom I've revealed my anxiety have been quite surprised, because I "always seem so chill," which never fails to make me laugh. Sometimes I feel so awful I'm sure I'm radiating bad vibes so palpable you can touch them. I'm very flattered when people think I'm a functional human being. I HAVE TRICKED YOU! YOU HAVE BEEN BAMBOOZLED, YOU LOVELY FOOL.

I've pretty much had to force myself into having a realistic sense of self-perception. This is incredibly annoying as it sounds like one of those flippant pieces of advice given by people who have never had any experience with mental illness; it's even more annoying because it works. Through a combination of practicing mindfulness and observing myself in a mirror for an absurd amount of time while repeating things like "you are fine, you deserve self-love, just chill out," I think I've developed a basic level of confidence. I still have moments where I feel like a repugnant piece of garbage, but nowhere near as often as I used to. Maybe 35 percent of the time now? Anything's better than 100 percent! Improvement!!

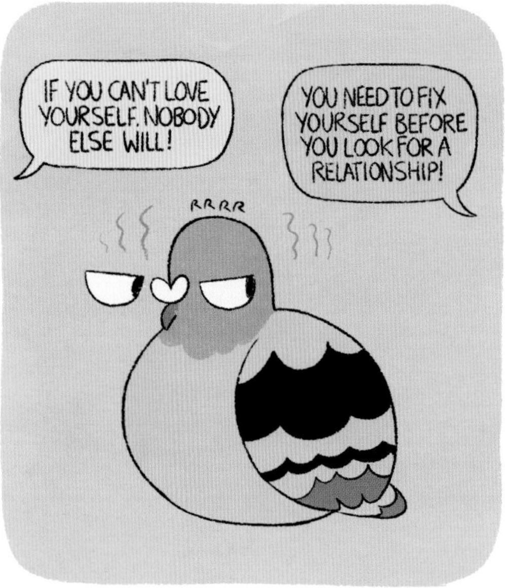
IF YOU CAN'T LOVE YOURSELF, NOBODY ELSE WILL!
YOU NEED TO FIX YOURSELF BEFORE YOU LOOK FOR A RELATIONSHIP!
RRRR

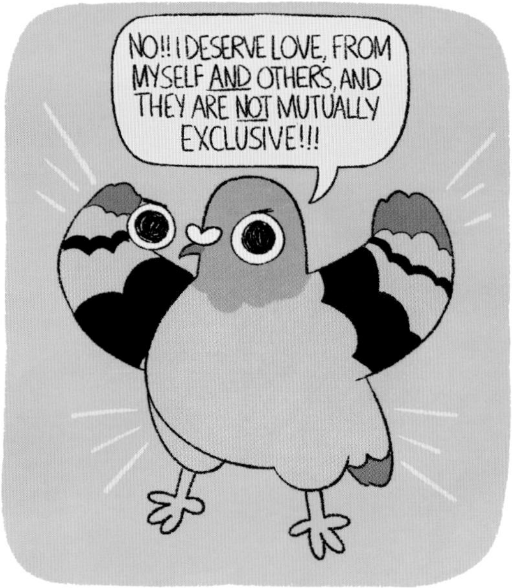
NO!! I DESERVE LOVE, FROM MYSELF AND OTHERS, AND THEY ARE NOT MUTUALLY EXCLUSIVE!!!

POSITIVITY

Being positive is something I still struggle with pretty much every day. It's become much, much easier than it used to be, but positivity is something I have to actively work toward and choose. Typing that made me shudder because it sounds like a cross-stitch picture you'd find in the home of someone who sells essential oils online.

My attitude toward optimism is a tempestuous one. A lot of my affirmative habits are actions that I absolutely hate being told to do by anybody else, because they're usually throwaway suggestions from people who don't understand the crushing reality of mental illness. Things like getting dressed even if I don't have the energy to go outside, or drinking more water, or taking a nice, long bath. These are all such easy steps toward improvement once you get going—it's just that getting started feels like scaling a mountain covered in butter.

It's true, even tiny things like taking care of your hygiene help a lot. But to actually get better, it's more important to deconstruct and rebuild how you fundamentally look at yourself and how you think, and that's not exactly a stroll in the park. When I say I've had to force myself to think more positively, I absolutely do not mean to come across as flippant; changing my thought patterns has been one of the most difficult endeavors I've ever taken on, and I'm still not great at it. I still have days where I just can't find anything good about myself or the world—and that's all right. Improvement isn't a straight line. The part of me that's incredibly petty and perfectionist loathes that getting better isn't a straightforward journey with checkpoints and prizes. *Please, brain, just give me a shot of serotonin whenever I'm doing good. I'm totally fine with being a Pavlovian dog. I want rewards! Gimme!*

Also, if you've gotten this far (thanks for not Frisbeeing this book into the bin), you'll know that I'm on medication, which has easily been one of the strongest influences on how I manage to navigate through life. Even after a year on meds, I still don't feel that comfortable talking about them in real life. I feel like people view them as cheating your way to happiness, when that's not really how it works. Medication is like an espresso shot for the brain; it gives me the energy I need to get started, but I'm still the one doing most of the legwork. Plus, even if there was a magical pill that made you happy, what would be wrong with taking that? I'd be on that instantly. Wait, that's probably MDMA. Never mind.

As I've also previously mentioned, medication isn't for everyone. It can be really frustrating constantly cycling through pills, suffering the barrage of side effects in the hope that it'll all turn out OK eventually. Different methods work for different people. I, for example, would rather set myself on fire than see another psychiatrist. Not because the doctor was bad, or anything, it just didn't work for me. Drawing dumb bird comics is my therapy, clearly.

I feel a bit weird trying to be all insightful about *my journey to improvement* because I still think I've got a good long way to go. Plus, my experience will never be the same as anyone else's. You might be reading this thinking I'm totally full of shit. I hope you're not, though. Regardless, this section isn't so much me preaching about How to Get Better (Have You Tried Lavender Oil?) but more about embracing the precious moments of positivity whenever they deign to appear. Some comics are about my rare bouts of body confidence; others are about how miraculous it is when you wake up and you just feel generally content.

After all the bullshit my own brain has subjected me to, I grab on to any good experience with my grubby, greedy hands and milk that baby till it's dry. When I'm down again, it helps a little to remember that I was happy for a bit at one point before, and it'll come again eventually. I hope these silly little pidges help you remember that, too.

SOME THINGS MIGHT NOT SEEM
THE MOST BEAUTIFUL AT FIRST...

BUT A LITTLE CARE CAN GO
A LONG WAY!!

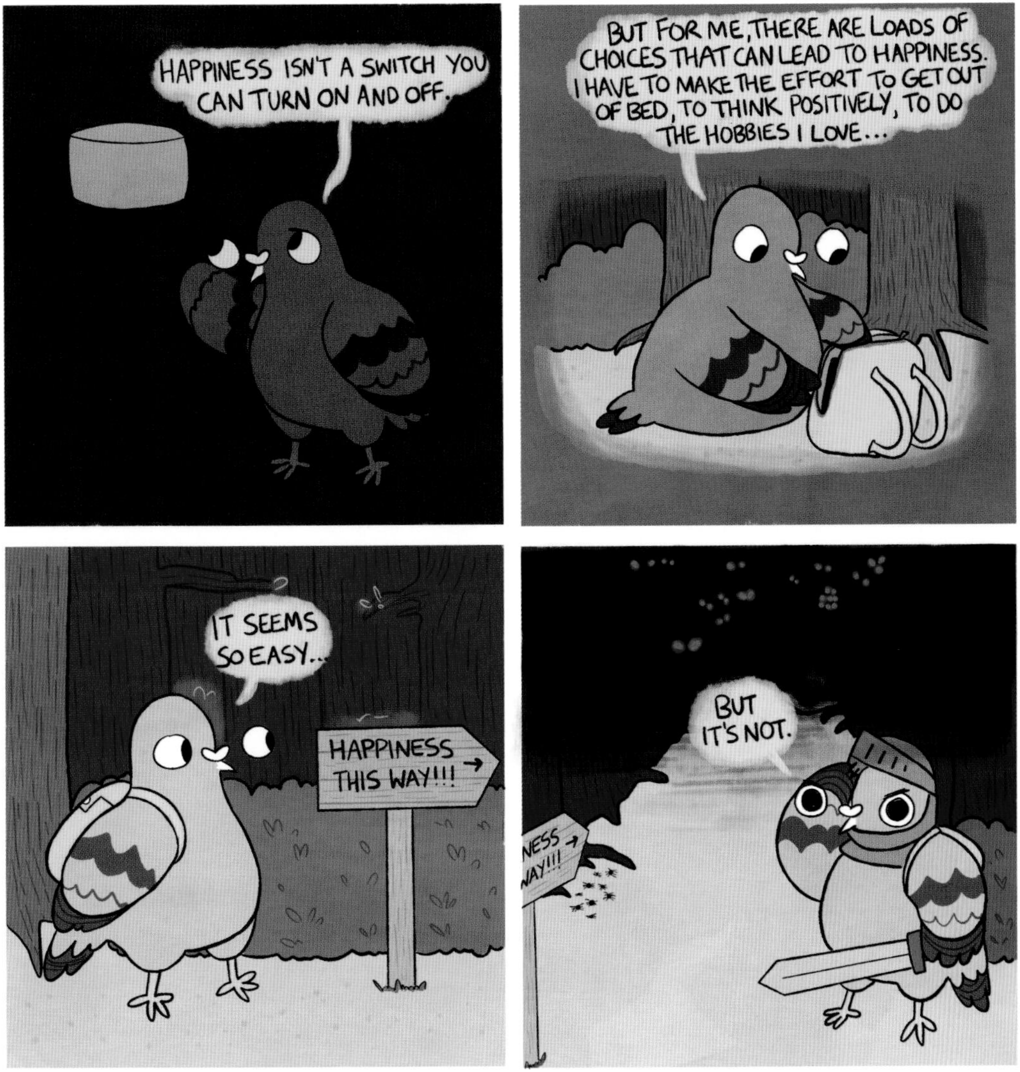
HAPPINESS ISN'T A SWITCH YOU CAN TURN ON AND OFF.
BUT FOR ME, THERE ARE LOADS OF CHOICES THAT CAN LEAD TO HAPPINESS. I HAVE TO MAKE THE EFFORT TO GET OUT OF BED, TO THINK POSITIVELY, TO DO THE HOBBIES I LOVE...
IT SEEMS SO EASY...
HAPPINESS THIS WAY!!! →
BUT IT'S NOT.

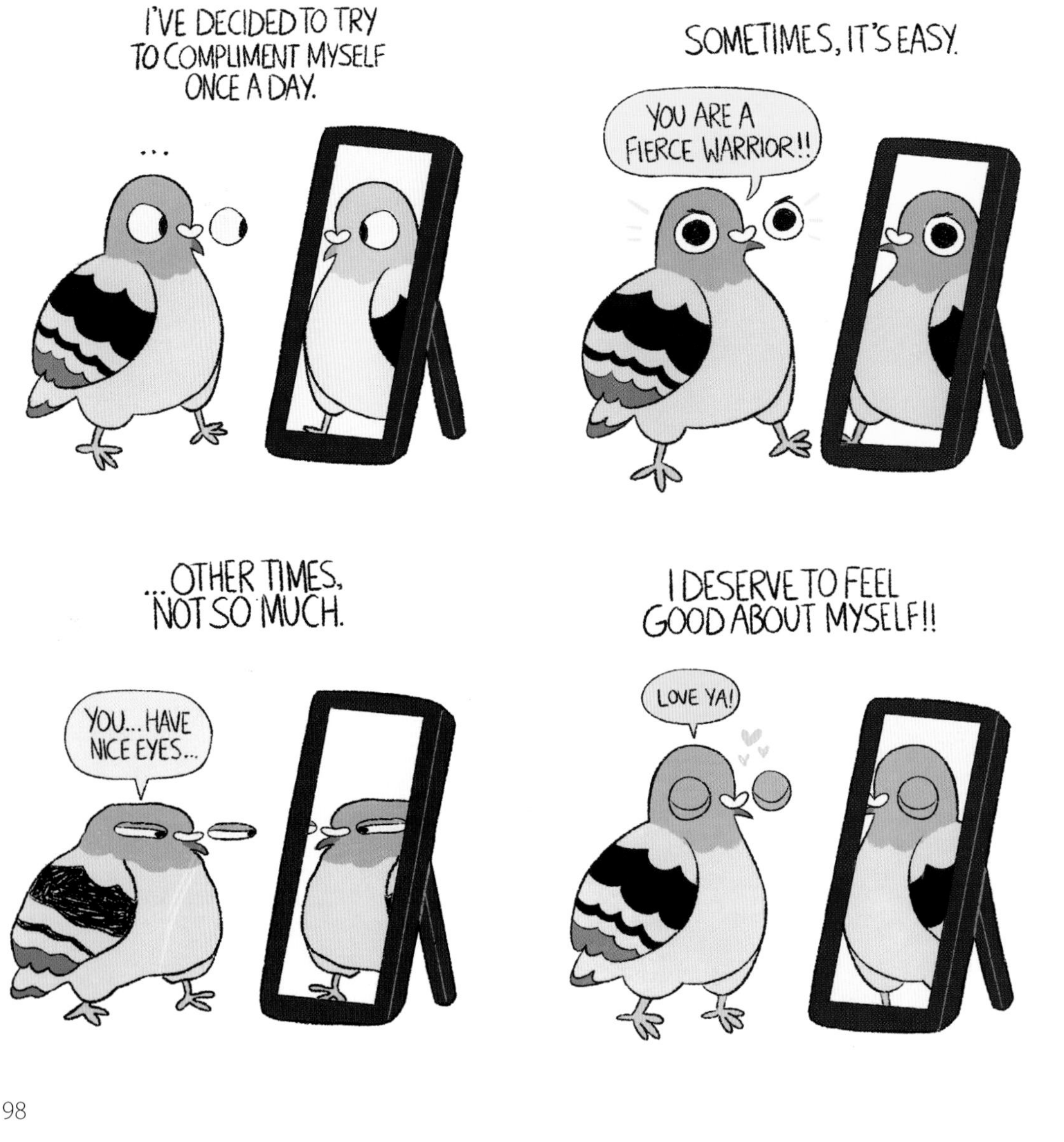
I'VE DECIDED TO TRY TO COMPLIMENT MYSELF ONCE A DAY.
...
SOMETIMES, IT'S EASY.
YOU ARE A FIERCE WARRIOR!!
...OTHER TIMES, NOT SO MUCH.
YOU... HAVE NICE EYES...
I DESERVE TO FEEL GOOD ABOUT MYSELF!!
LOVE YA!

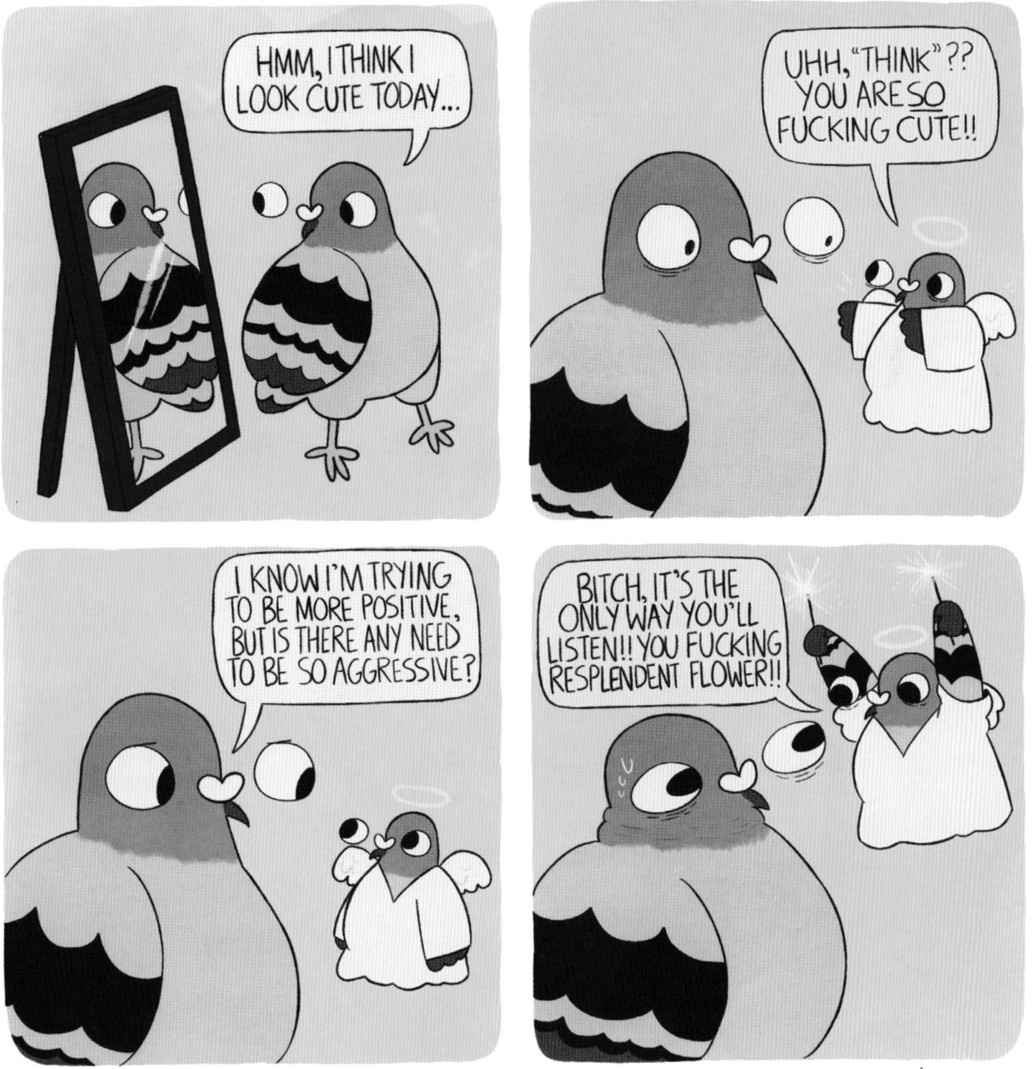
HMM, I THINK I LOOK CUTE TODAY...
UHH, "THINK"?? YOU ARE SO FUCKING CUTE!!
I KNOW I'M TRYING TO BE MORE POSITIVE, BUT IS THERE ANY NEED TO BE SO AGGRESSIVE?
BITCH, IT'S THE ONLY WAY YOU'LL LISTEN!! YOU FUCKING RESPLENDENT FLOWER!!

I AM NO LONGER WORRYING IF SOMETHING WILL SUIT ME OR NOT.

IF I LIKE IT, THEN IT SUITS ME AUTOMATICALLY!

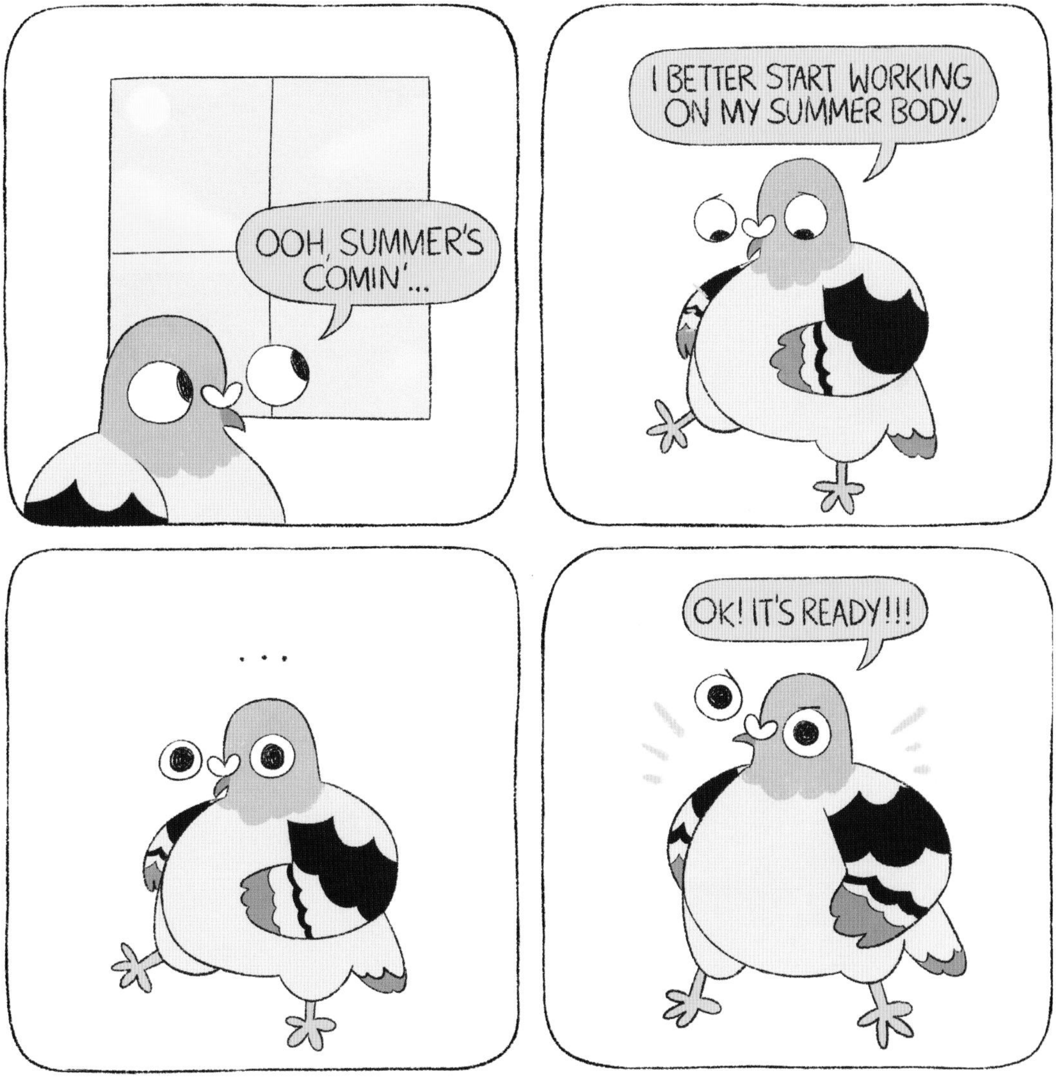
OOH, SUMMER'S COMIN'...
I BETTER START WORKING ON MY SUMMER BODY.
...
OK! IT'S READY!!!

Like pretty much everybody who has ever traversed adolescence, I've suffered through the horrors of acne. My body obviously relishes prolonging my suffering, as I continued to be plagued with spots into my twenties. Not just on my face, either, but on my chest and all down my back. It was as if I'd been flicked with a bright red paintbrush all over. As you can imagine, this didn't do wonders for my already tremulous confidence.

Being secure in your appearance doesn't automatically equate to having a healthy mind, but it certainly bloody helps. It's one thing battling the negative thoughts that you know have no basis in reality; it's a whole other ordeal when your looks are afflicted by something that's deemed hideous by society's standards. Feeling shitty about my skin was the nail in the coffin when it came to justifying my anxiety and depression. I felt ugly inside and out. I really got dealt an awful hand in the game of genetics, didn't I? Thanks, Mum and Dad.

Convincing myself that I was deserving of self-love even if I looked like a bright red mountain range was almost impossible. My acne is largely under control now, but every mini-breakout still causes me mild panic. But then I remember that I would still care for all my loved ones even if they had a case of pizza face, so I should extend myself the same courtesy. I also don't care if random people in the street have a spotty forehead, so why should I worry about what they think about me? Oh, what's that? Marie in the grocery store is grossed out by my skin? Big deal. Mind your business, Marie. Get back to perusing the hummus.

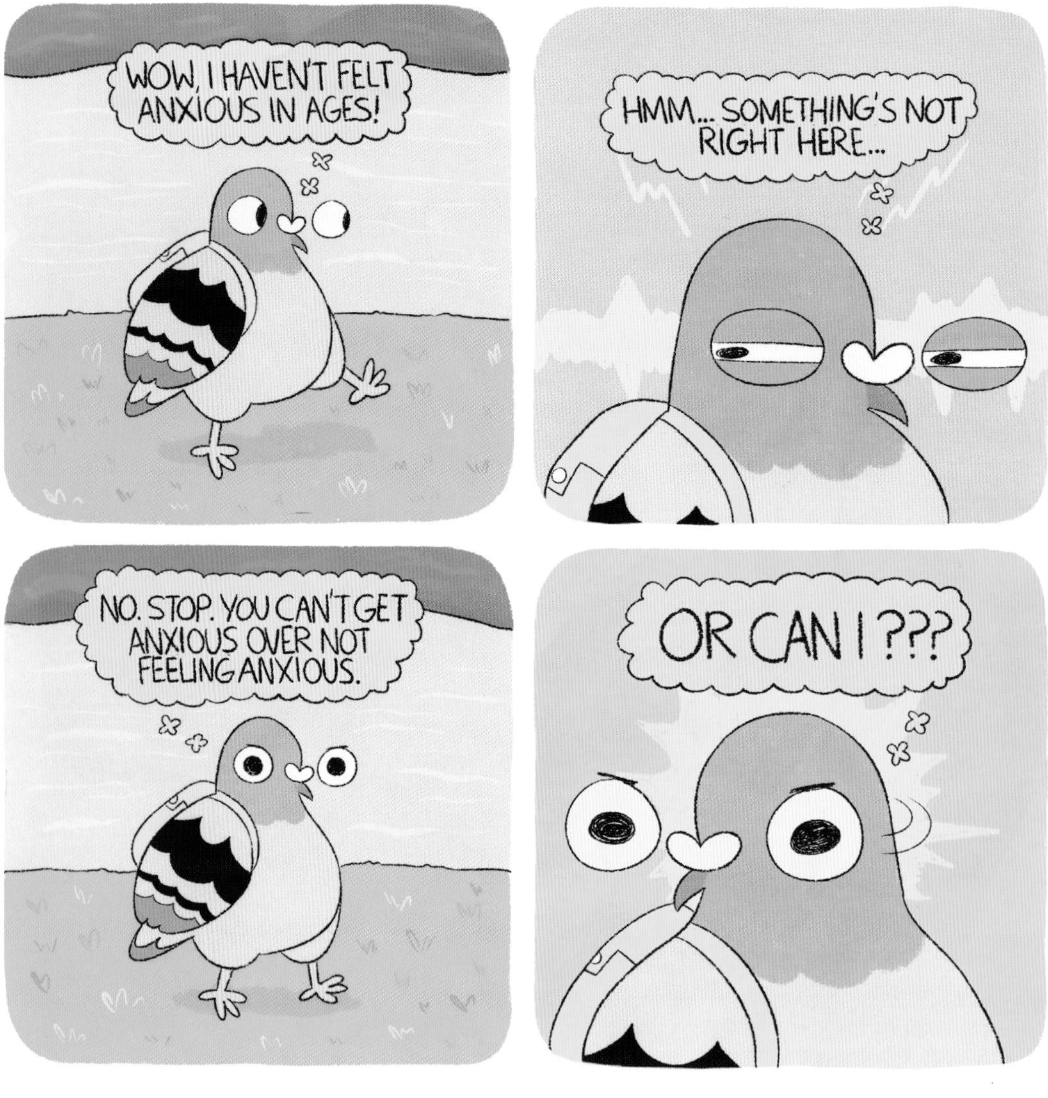
WOW, I HAVEN'T FELT ANXIOUS IN AGES!
HMM... SOMETHING'S NOT RIGHT HERE...
NO. STOP. YOU CAN'T GET ANXIOUS OVER NOT FEELING ANXIOUS.
OR CAN I???

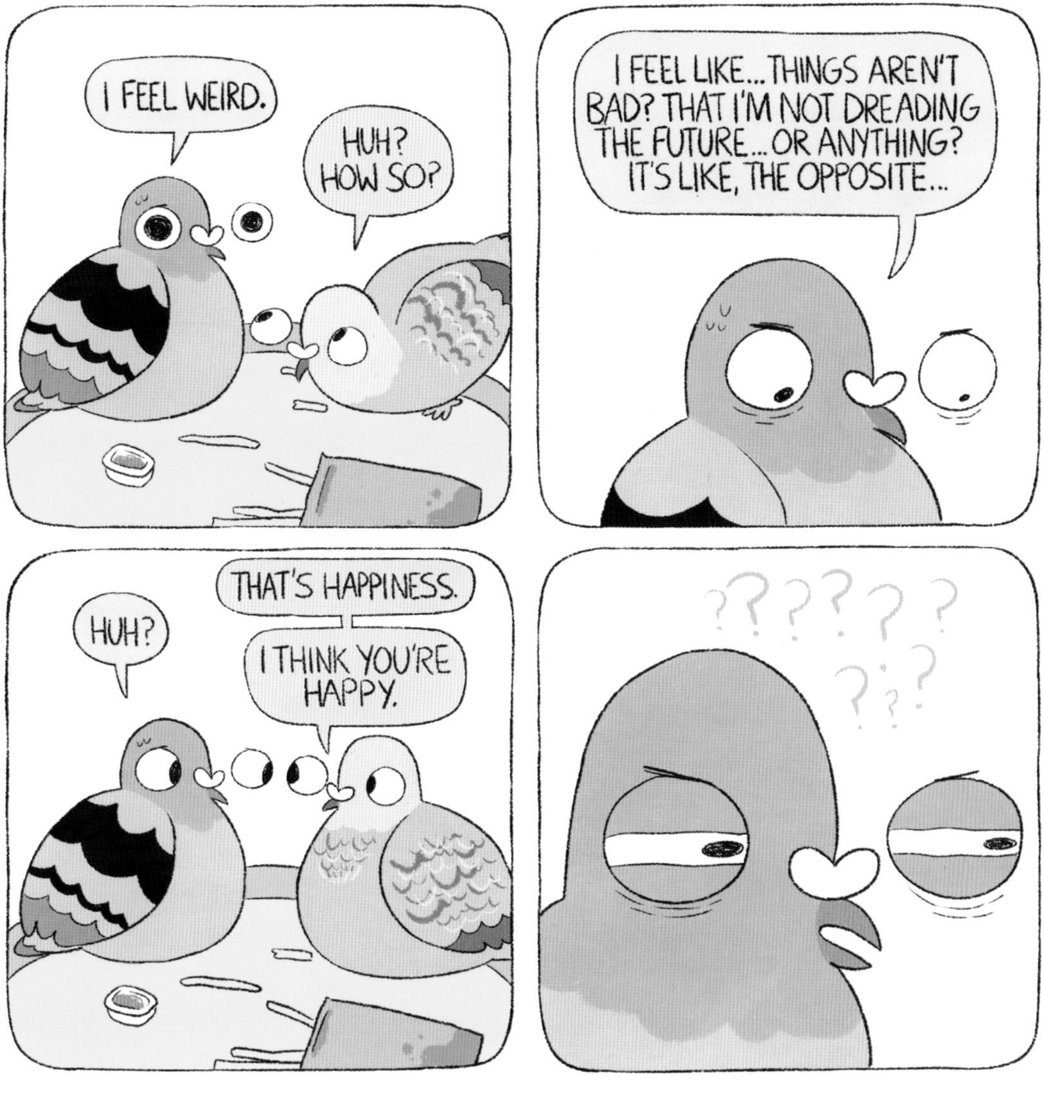
I FEEL WEIRD.
HUH? HOW SO?
I FEEL LIKE... THINGS AREN'T BAD? THAT I'M NOT DREADING THE FUTURE... OR ANYTHING? IT'S LIKE, THE OPPOSITE...
HUH?
THAT'S HAPPINESS.
I THINK YOU'RE HAPPY.

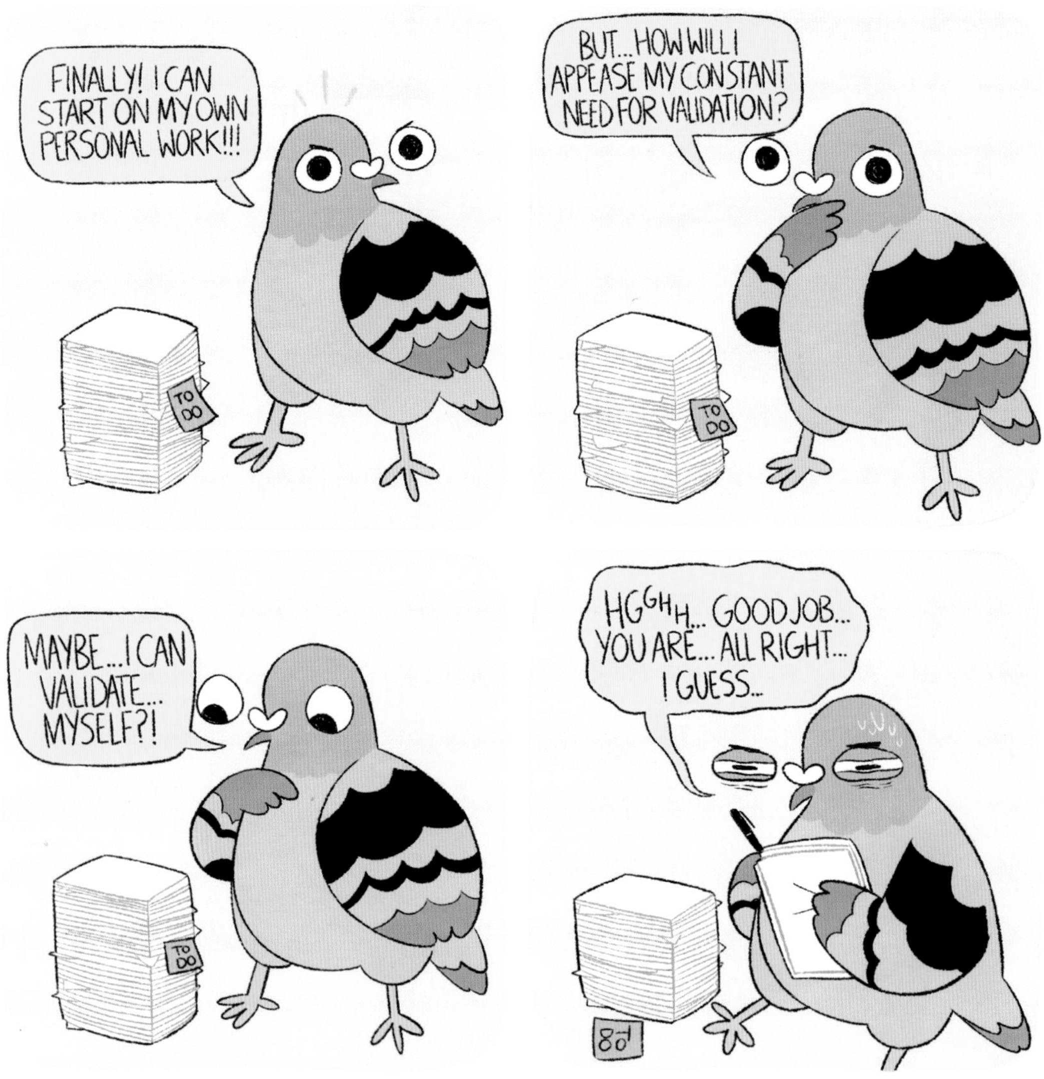
FINALLY! I CAN START ON MY OWN PERSONAL WORK!!!
TO DO
BUT... HOW WILL I APPEASE MY CONSTANT NEED FOR VALIDATION?
TO DO
MAYBE... I CAN VALIDATE... MYSELF?!
TO DO
HGGHH... GOOD JOB... YOU ARE... ALL RIGHT... I GUESS...

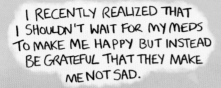

I RECENTLY REALIZED THAT I SHOULDN'T WAIT FOR MY MEDS TO MAKE ME HAPPY BUT INSTEAD BE GRATEFUL THAT THEY MAKE ME NOT SAD.

I'M TRYING TO BE RESPONSIBLE FOR MY HAPPINESS.

IT'S HARD...

IT'S TAKING AWHILE...

BUT I THINK I'M GETTING GOOD AT IT!

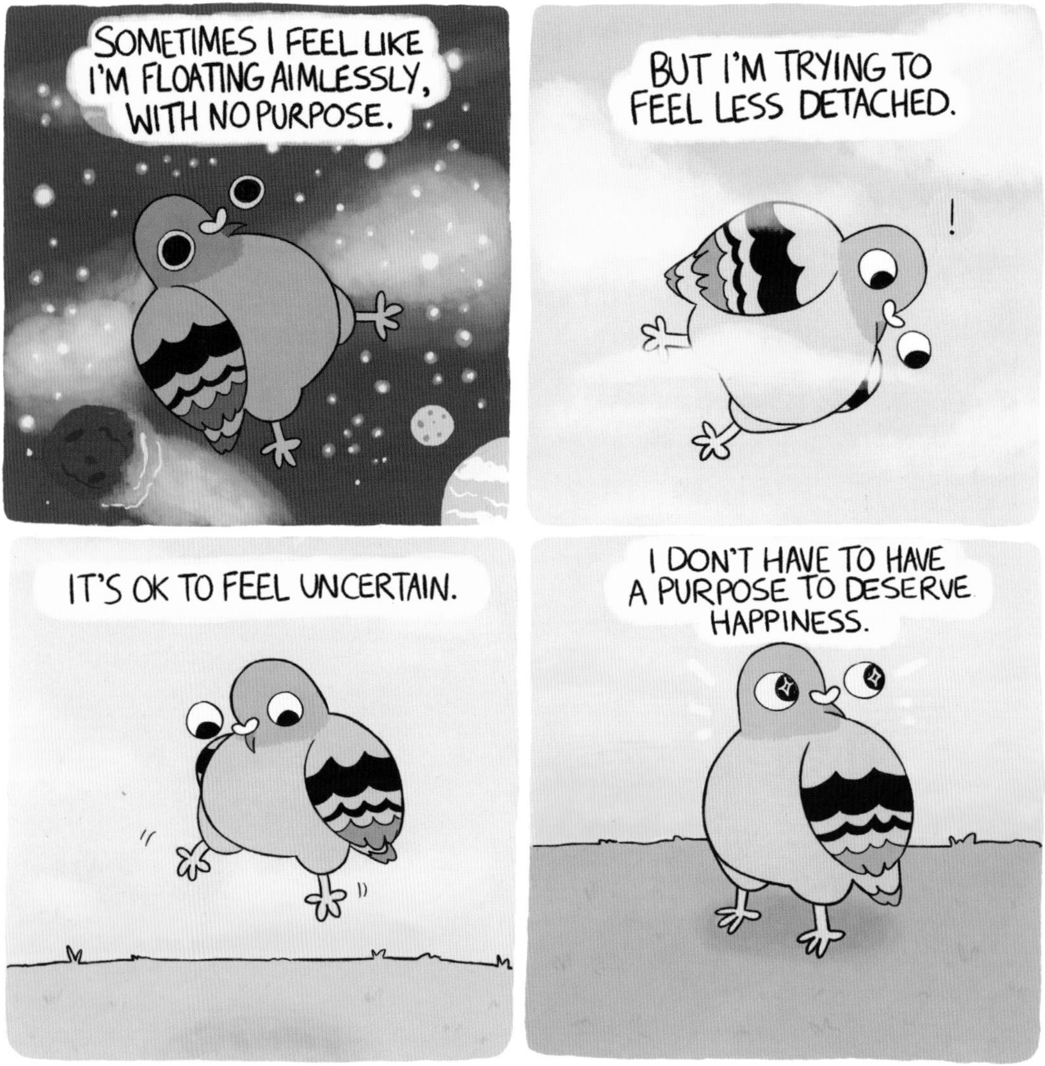
SOMETIMES I FEEL LIKE I'M FLOATING AIMLESSLY, WITH NO PURPOSE.
BUT I'M TRYING TO FEEL LESS DETACHED.
!
IT'S OK TO FEEL UNCERTAIN.
I DON'T HAVE TO HAVE A PURPOSE TO DESERVE HAPPINESS.

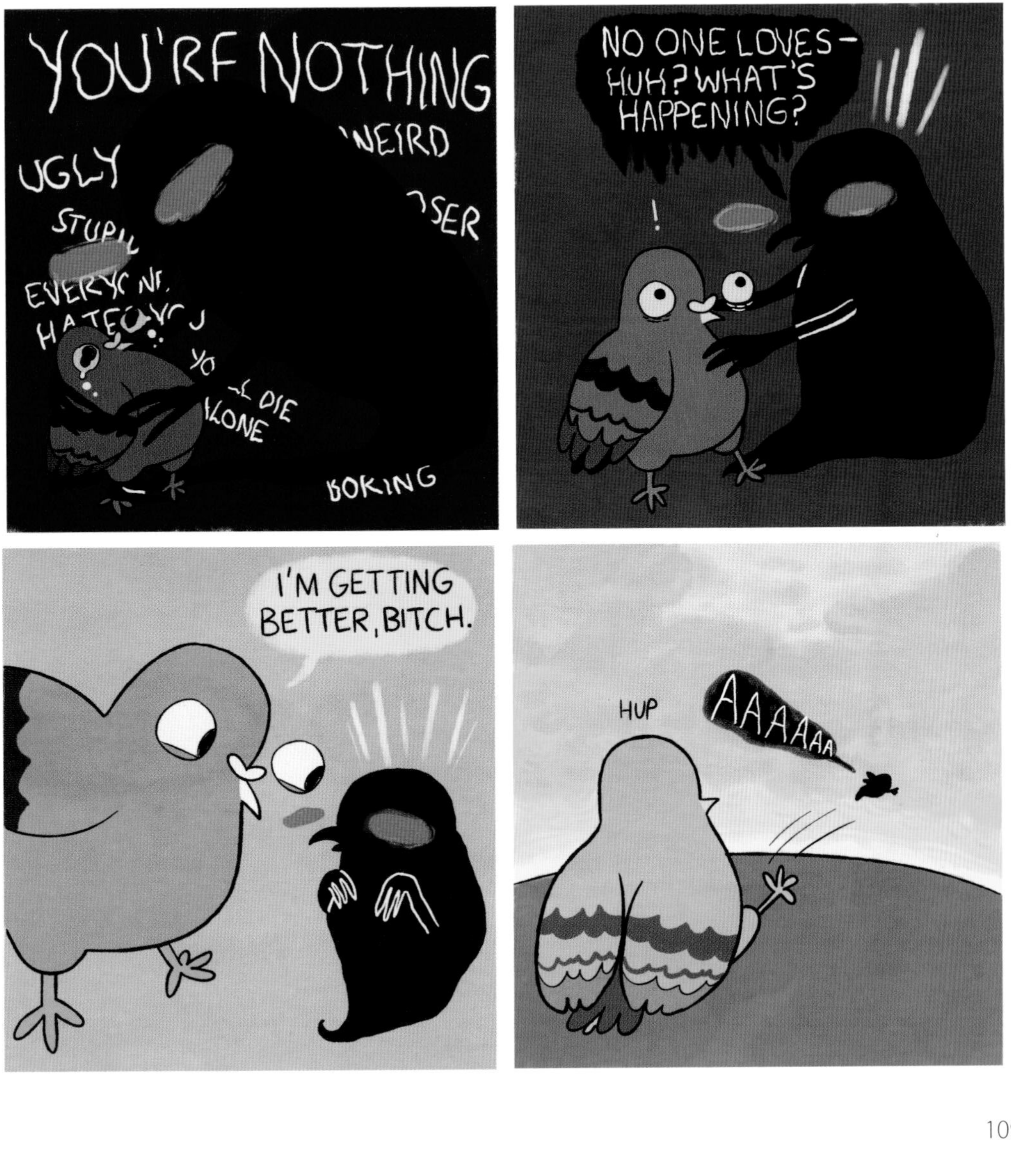
YOU'RF NOTHING
UGLY
WEIRD
STUPI
SER
DIE
LONE
BOKING
NO ONE LOVES-
HUH? WHAT'S HAPPENING?
!
I'M GETTING BETTER, BITCH.
HUP
AAAAAA

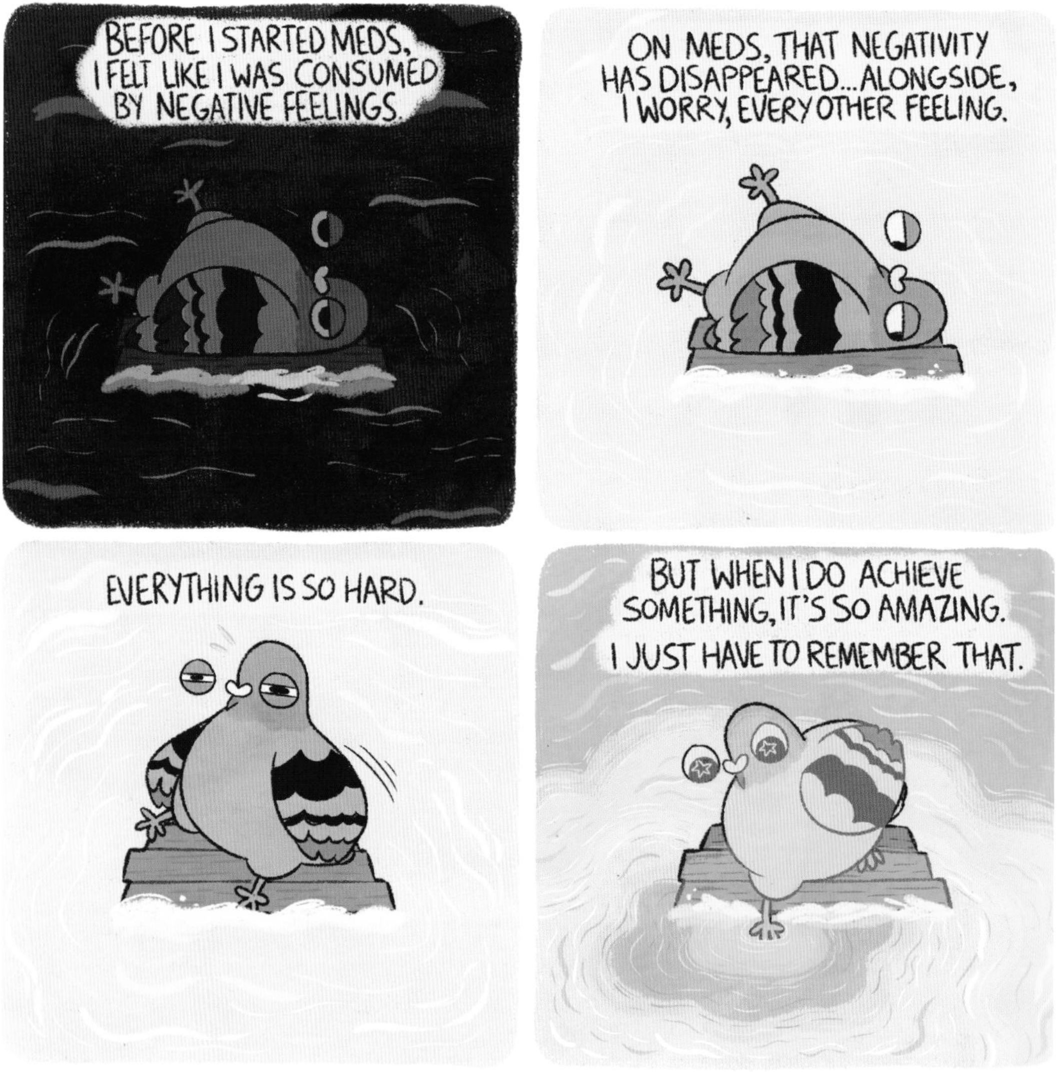
BEFORE I STARTED MEDS, I FELT LIKE I WAS CONSUMED BY NEGATIVE FEELINGS.
ON MEDS, THAT NEGATIVITY HAS DISAPPEARED... ALONGSIDE, I WORRY, EVERY OTHER FEELING.
EVERYTHING IS SO HARD.
BUT WHEN I DO ACHIEVE SOMETHING, IT'S SO AMAZING.
I JUST HAVE TO REMEMBER THAT.

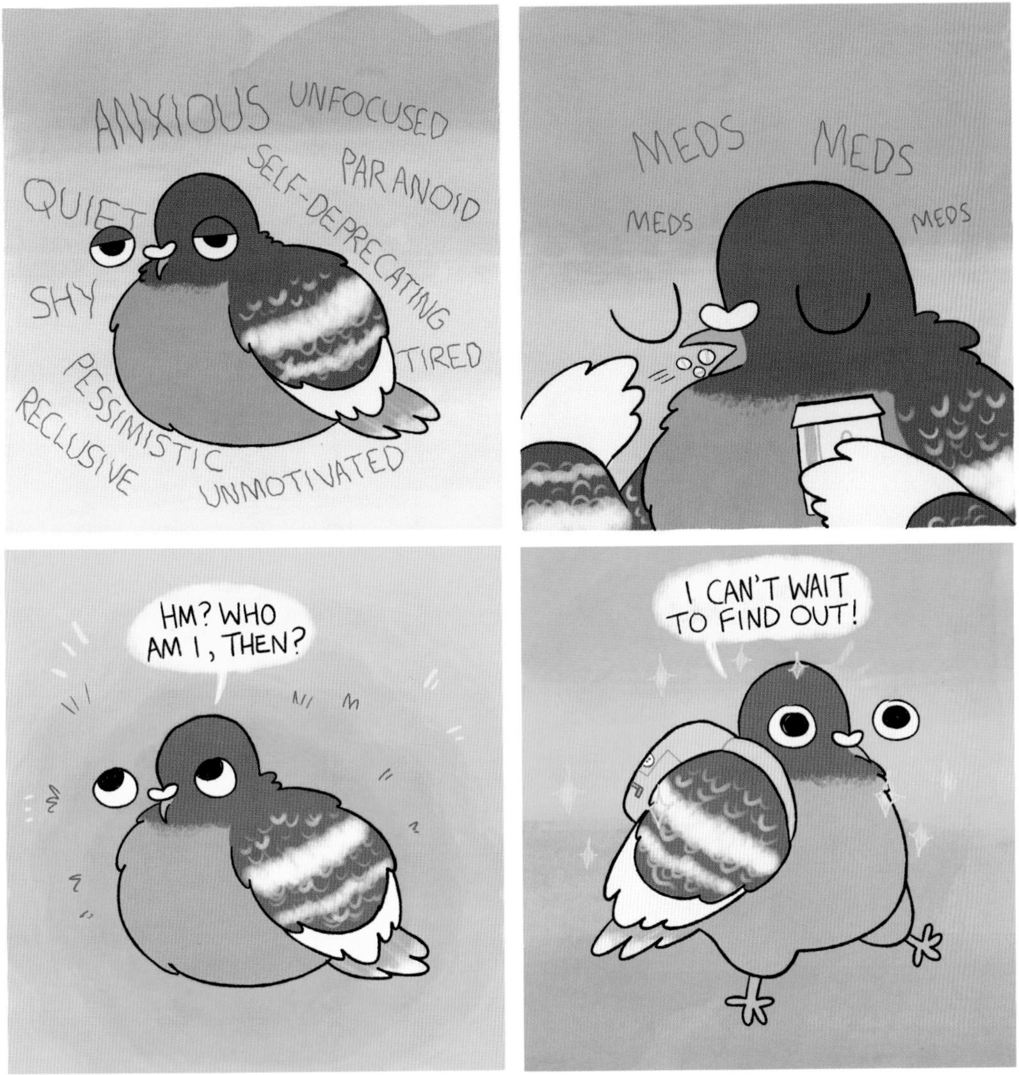
ANXIOUS
UNFOCUSED
PARANOID
QUIET
SELF-DEPRECATING
SHY
TIRED
PESSIMISTIC
RECLUSIVE
UNMOTIVATED
MEDS
MEDS
MEDS
MEDS
HM? WHO AM I, THEN?
I CAN'T WAIT TO FIND OUT!

AS EARLY AS I CAN REMEMBER, OTHERS
SEEMED SO CONFIDENT IN THEMSELVES.

I THOUGHT I WAS JUST A LATE BLOOMER,
BUT AS I GOT OLDER, OTHERS STILL SEEMED
MILES AHEAD OF ME.

BUT THE ONLY ONE
I SHOULD COMPARE
MYSELF TO IS ME!

I'M STILL GROWING, BUT
I'VE COME SO FAR!!

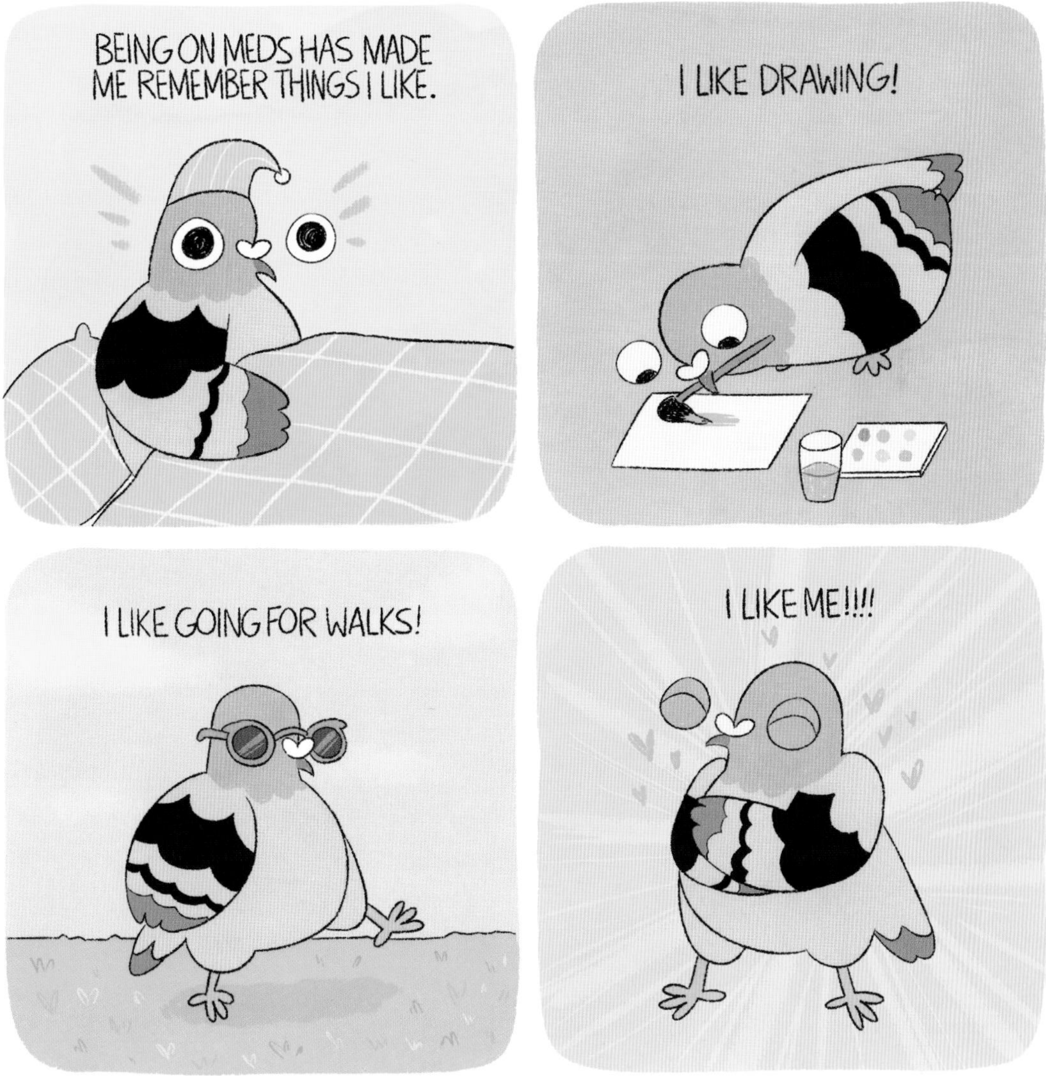
BEING ON MEDS HAS MADE ME REMEMBER THINGS I LIKE.
I LIKE DRAWING!
I LIKE GOING FOR WALKS!
I LIKE ME!!!!

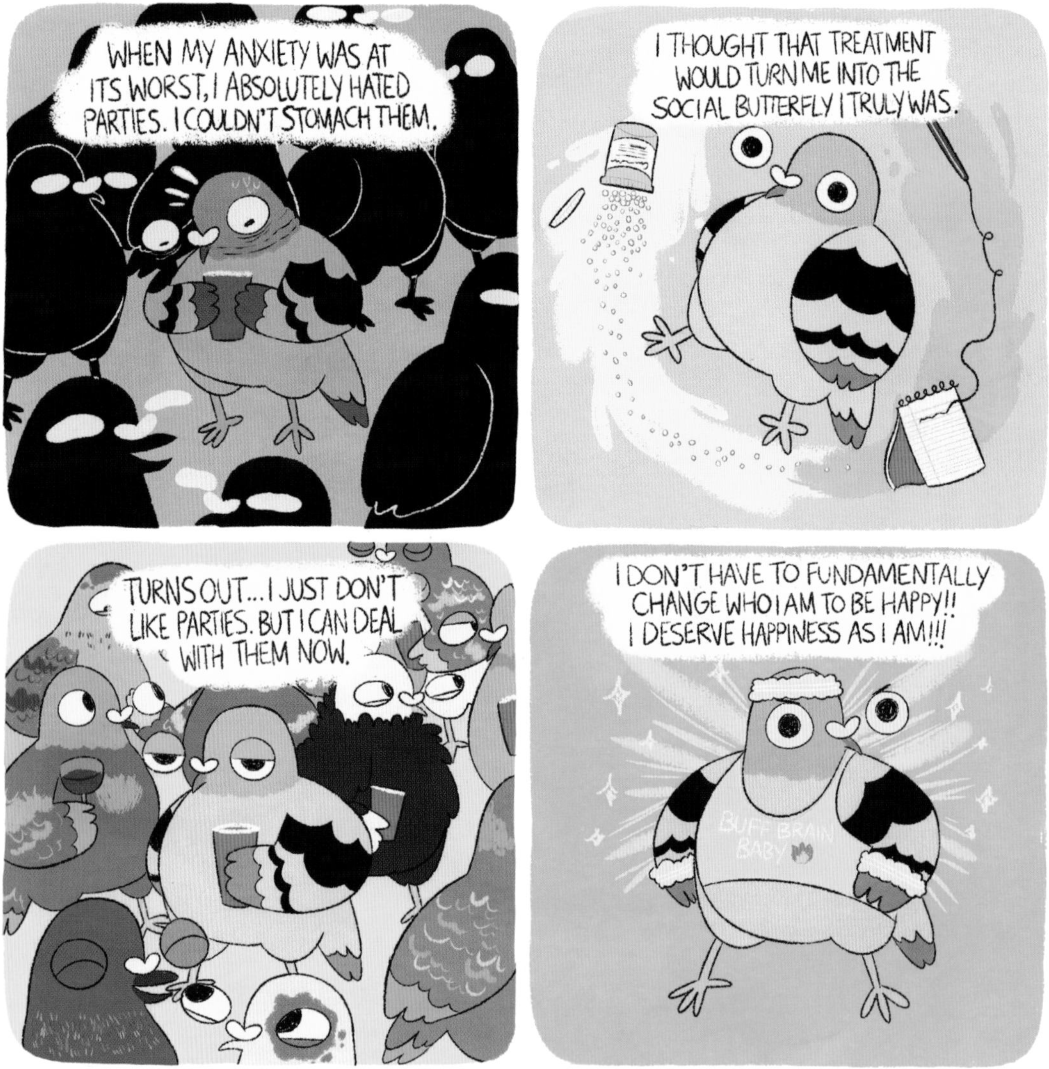
WHEN MY ANXIETY WAS AT ITS WORST, I ABSOLUTELY HATED PARTIES. I COULDN'T STOMACH THEM.
I THOUGHT THAT TREATMENT WOULD TURN ME INTO THE SOCIAL BUTTERFLY I TRULY WAS.
TURNS OUT... I JUST DON'T LIKE PARTIES. BUT I CAN DEAL WITH THEM NOW.
I DON'T HAVE TO FUNDAMENTALLY CHANGE WHO I AM TO BE HAPPY!! I DESERVE HAPPINESS AS I AM!!!
BUFF BRAIN BABY

I KNOW THAT I CAN BE REALLY HARD ON MYSELF...
WEIRD
CLINGY
LAZY
ANNOYING
LOSER
AWKWARD
UGLY
EMOTIONAL
BORING
I STRUGGLE TO SEE WHAT OTHERS CAN.
UNIQUE
TALENTED
CUTE
SWEET
FUNNY
I'M REALLY TRYING TO LOVE MYSELF.
I AM...
FAILURE
SELF-OBSESSED
STUPID
I THINK I'M GETTING THERE.
KINDA FUNNY!!!
I GUESS!!

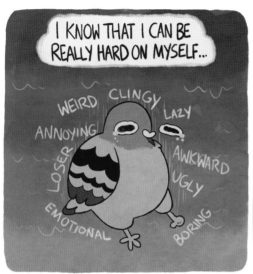

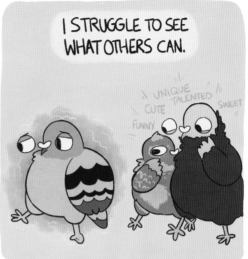

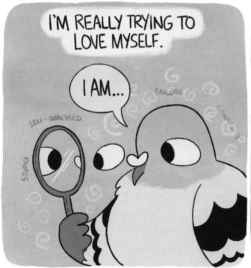

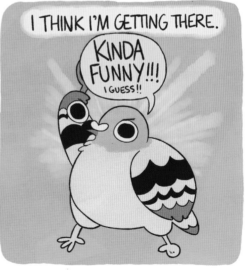

AAH, I'VE BEEN INVITED TO AN EVENT TONIGHT, BUT I REALLY DON'T WANT TO GO...
31 FRI
SO I WON'T! I'M ALLOWED TO SAY NO TO PROTECT MY MENTAL HEALTH!!

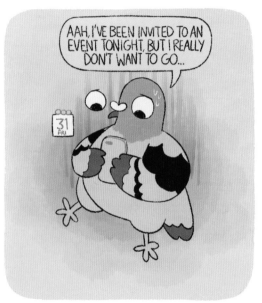

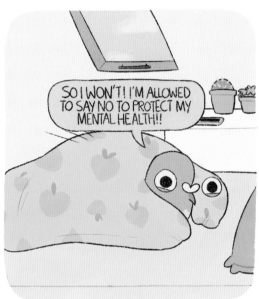

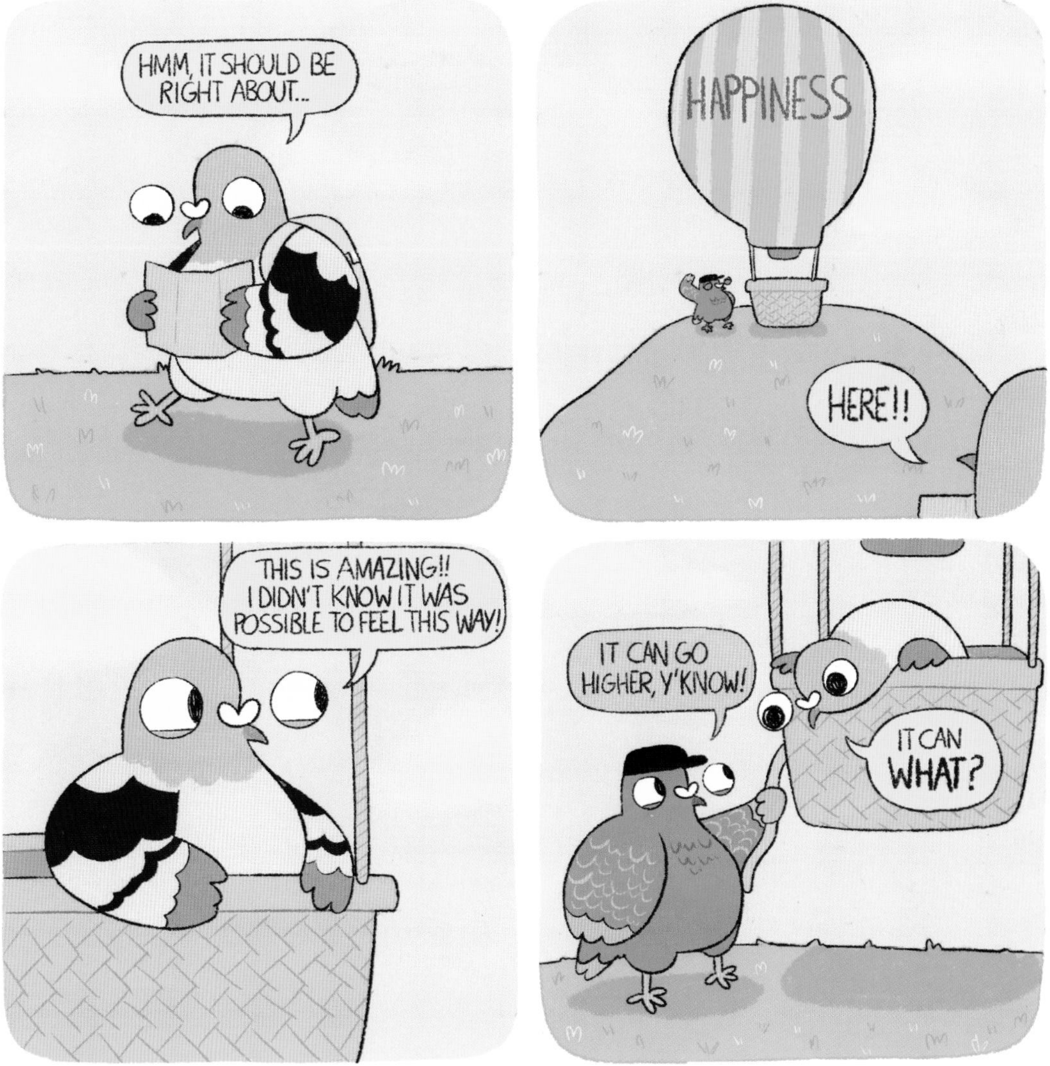
HMM, IT SHOULD BE RIGHT ABOUT...
HAPPINESS
HERE!!
THIS IS AMAZING!! I DIDN'T KNOW IT WAS POSSIBLE TO FEEL THIS WAY!
IT CAN GO HIGHER, Y'KNOW!
IT CAN WHAT?

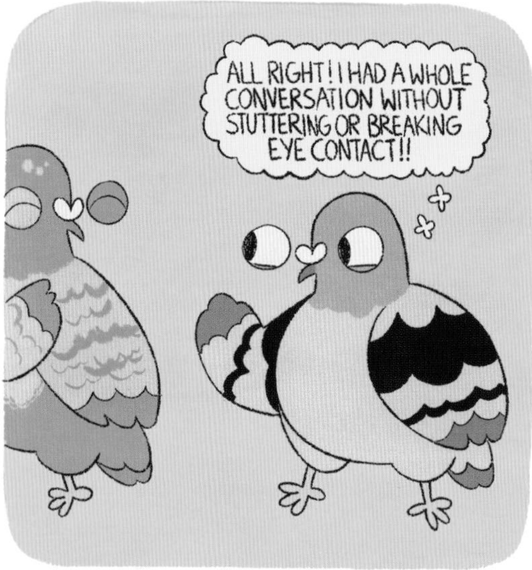
ALL RIGHT! I HAD A WHOLE CONVERSATION WITHOUT STUTTERING OR BREAKING EYE CONTACT!!

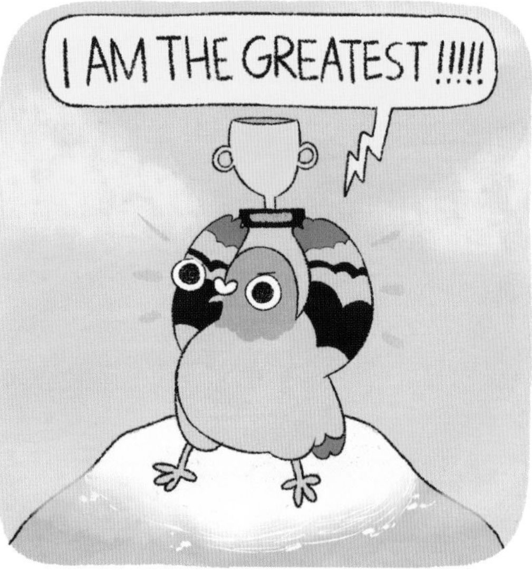
I AM THE GREATEST !!!!!

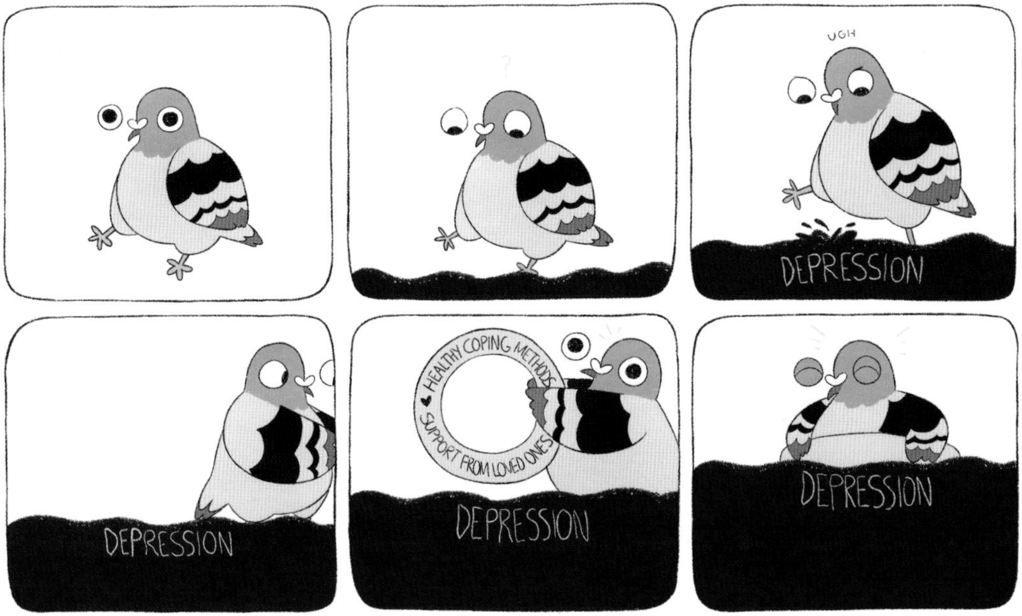
?
UGH
DEPRESSION
DEPRESSION
HEALTHY COPING METHODS
SUPPORT FROM LOVED ONES
DEPRESSION
DEPRESSION

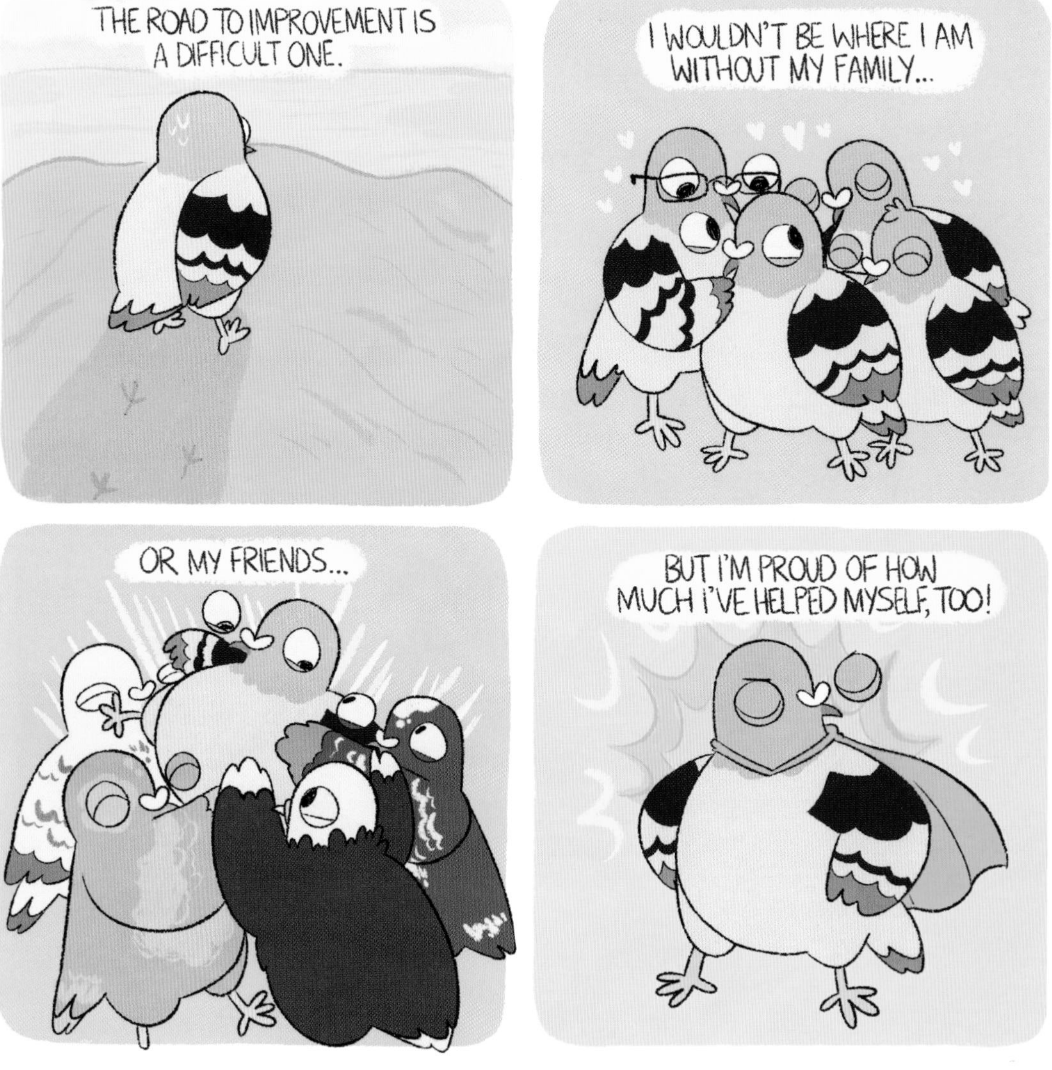
THE ROAD TO IMPROVEMENT IS A DIFFICULT ONE.
I WOULDN'T BE WHERE I AM WITHOUT MY FAMILY...
OR MY FRIENDS...
BUT I'M PROUD OF HOW MUCH I'VE HELPED MYSELF, TOO!

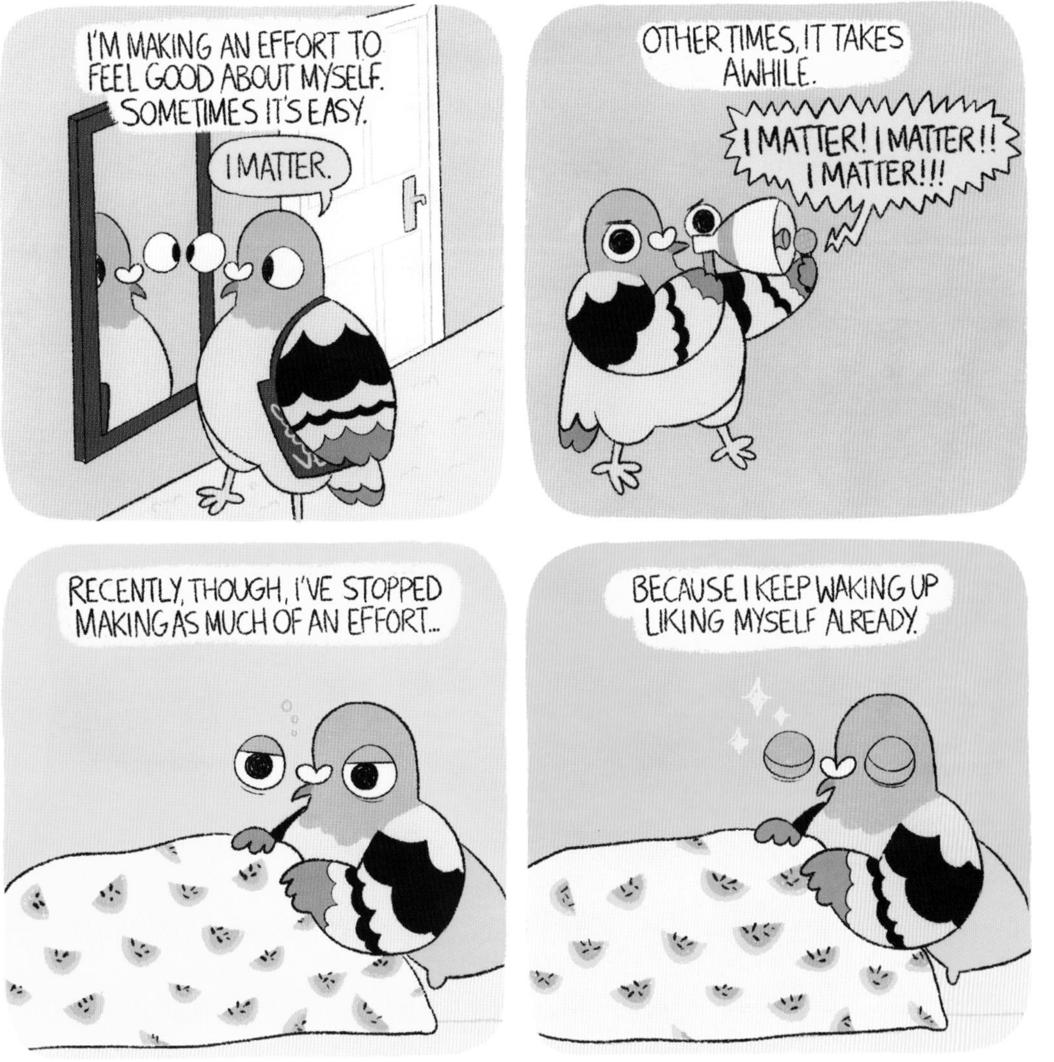
I'M MAKING AN EFFORT TO FEEL GOOD ABOUT MYSELF. SOMETIMES IT'S EASY.
I MATTER.
OTHER TIMES, IT TAKES AWHILE.
I MATTER! I MATTER!! I MATTER!!!
RECENTLY, THOUGH, I'VE STOPPED MAKING AS MUCH OF AN EFFORT...
BECAUSE I KEEP WAKING UP LIKING MYSELF ALREADY.

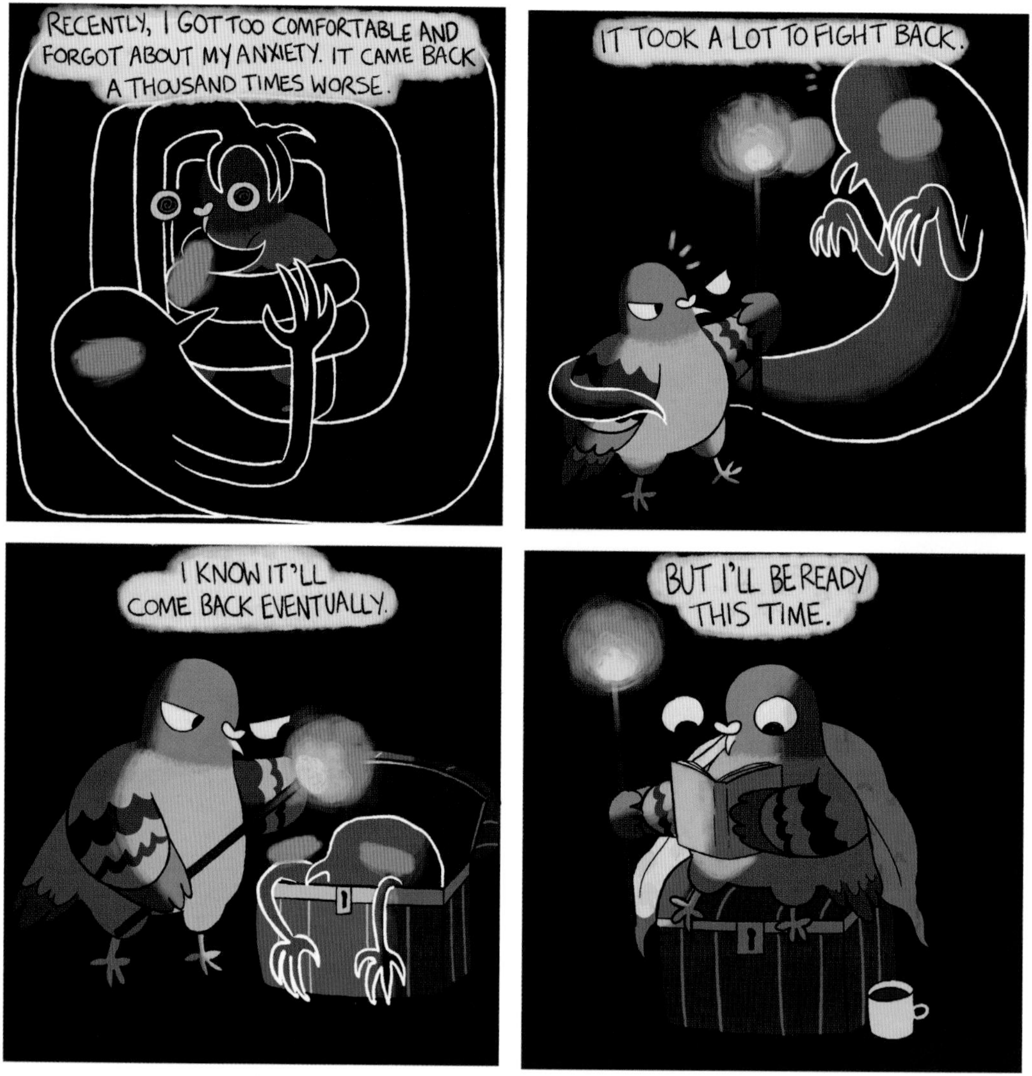
RECENTLY, I GOT TOO COMFORTABLE AND FORGOT ABOUT MY ANXIETY. IT CAME BACK A THOUSAND TIMES WORSE.
IT TOOK A LOT TO FIGHT BACK.
I KNOW IT'LL COME BACK EVENTUALLY.
BUT I'LL BE READY THIS TIME.

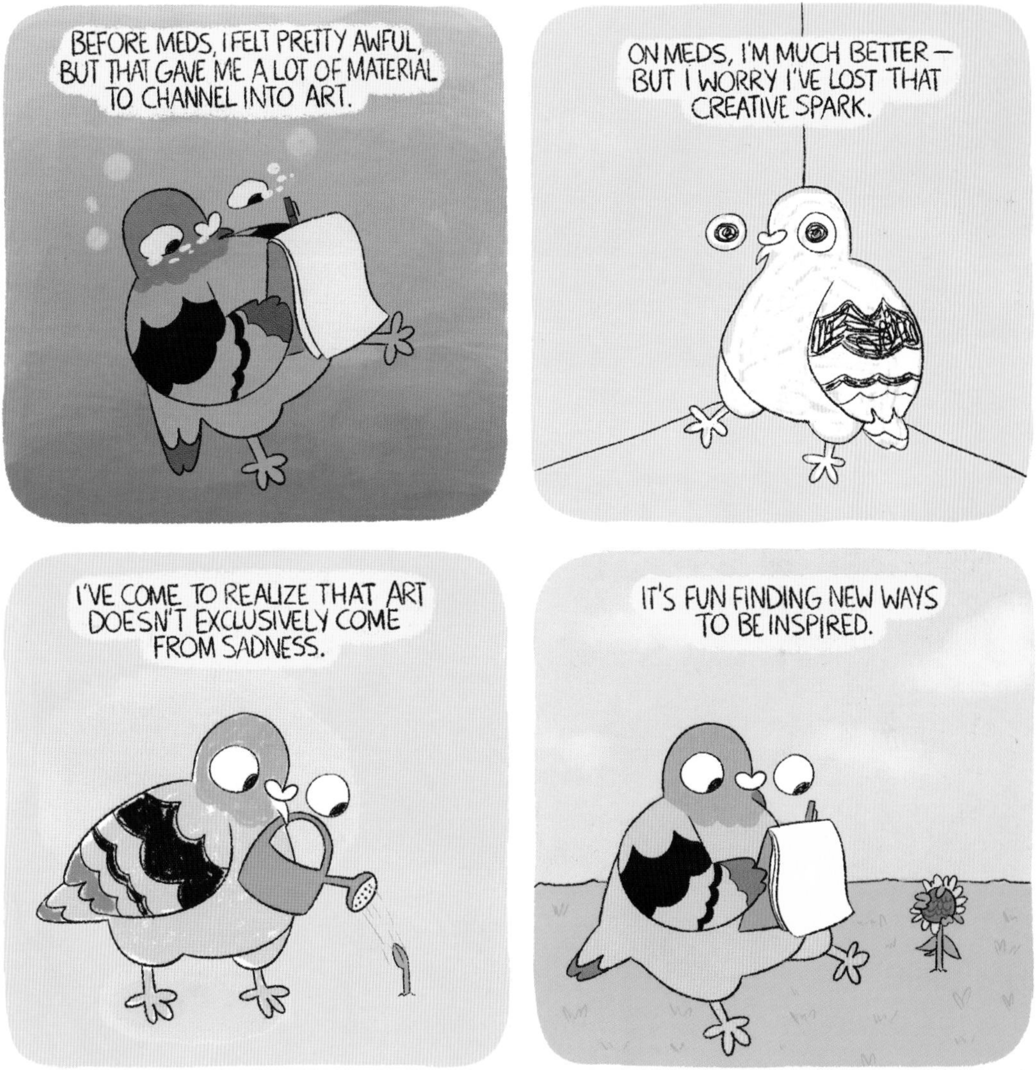
BEFORE MEDS, I FELT PRETTY AWFUL, BUT THAT GAVE ME A LOT OF MATERIAL TO CHANNEL INTO ART.
ON MEDS, I'M MUCH BETTER— BUT I WORRY I'VE LOST THAT CREATIVE SPARK.
I'VE COME TO REALIZE THAT ART DOESN'T EXCLUSIVELY COME FROM SADNESS.
IT'S FUN FINDING NEW WAYS TO BE INSPIRED.

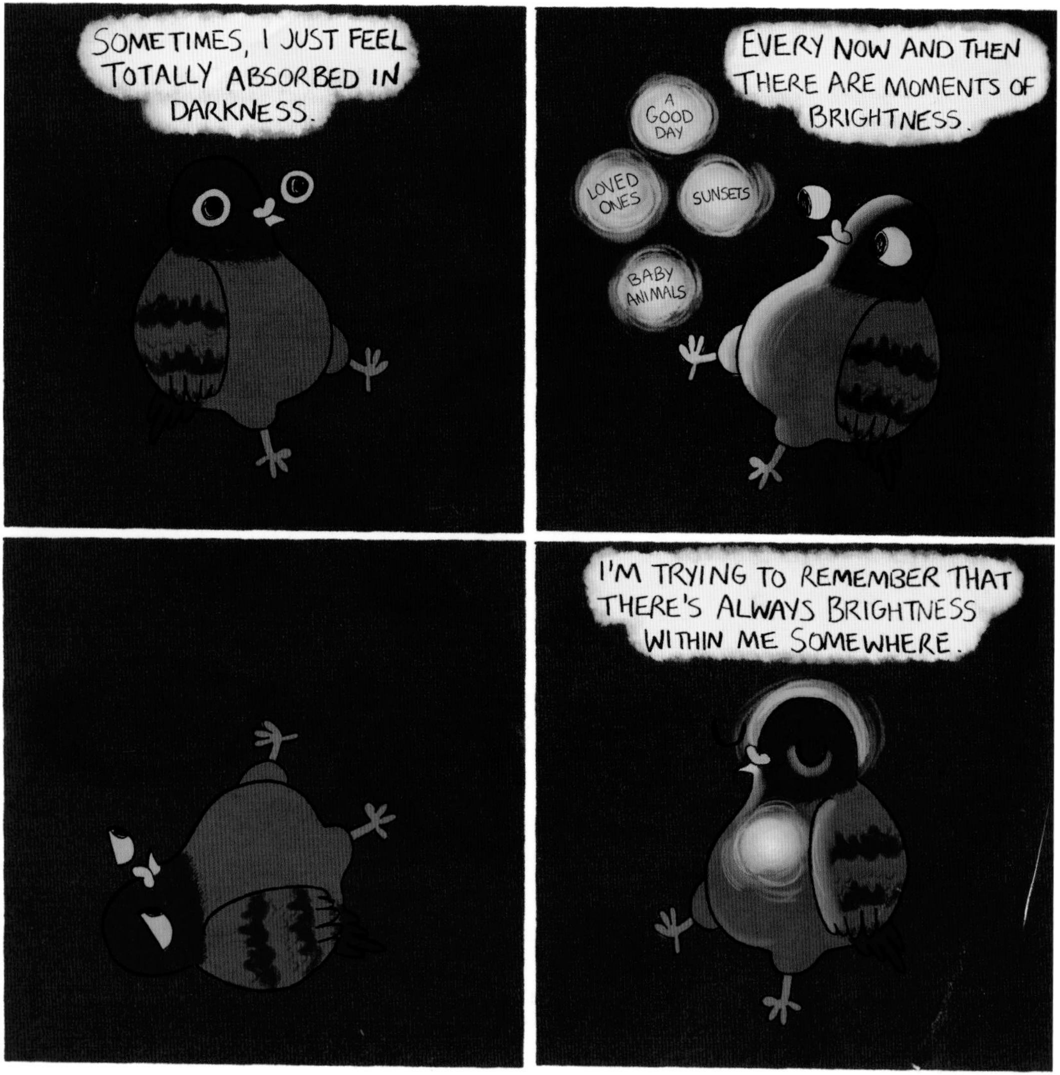
SOMETIMES, I JUST FEEL TOTALLY ABSORBED IN DARKNESS.
EVERY NOW AND THEN THERE ARE MOMENTS OF BRIGHTNESS.
A GOOD DAY
LOVED ONES
SUNSETS
BABY ANIMALS
I'M TRYING TO REMEMBER THAT THERE'S ALWAYS BRIGHTNESS WITHIN ME SOMEWHERE.

CONCLUSION

The entire time I've been working on this book, I've been completely at a loss over how I'd end it. Guess my degree in English literature was a complete waste, then. I can spew out a concise conclusion after 10,000 words on postmodernist theory with no problem. Nicely wrapping up the most soul-baring and personal piece of work I'll probably ever make, though? Nah. Can't do it. I want my tuition back, please.

But the more I thought about it, the more I realized how fitting it was that I didn't know how to finish this, because my mental illness hasn't just ended. Things have most definitely improved, of course, but improvement is a process that I have to constantly strive for. I didn't start popping pills and suddenly my whole life was fixed; every day is an uphill struggle, and sometimes I worry that there's nothing at the top and I'm just going to keep climbing forever. That's another aspect of getting better that I wasn't really prepared for—just how much I was going to have to force myself to do things I really didn't want to do. It's especially annoying considering that it's the go-to advice from morons who don't get mental illness: "Just be happy! Just get out of bed! Just *do it!*" As if I'd never thought of that before! Wow! The truth is, however, that bullshit has a nugget of truth; it's just usually wrapped in a terrible attitude when other people say it.

Some days I still have to force myself to get out of bed. Force myself to get dressed. Force myself to go to work. To make conversation, to eat something other than toast and ice cream, to take care of my hygiene. Basic things that most people take for granted. Even then, "just do it" isn't an absolute solution. There are so many fine lines to tread and so many things to juggle. Force yourself to do things, but don't burn yourself out. Push yourself out of your comfort zone, but respect your limits. Indulge yourself in sadness occasionally, but don't let it consume you. In many respects, it's like I've traded one draining way of life for another. The difference is, all of this eventually pays off, and it's so, so worth it.

I've stopped looking at getting better as solely an end goal to strive toward; instead, it's a process that you have to relish in all its minutiae. Celebrate all the small things, like going so many days without a breakdown, or managing a night out when you don't want to go home early. I suspect that if I'm holding out for the day when I'll have anxiety for the last time, I'll be waiting for a good long while.

Some people do manage to completely move past their anxiety and depression, looking back on those days as a dark period of their life, but one that is firmly in the past. This certainly does not invalidate their experiences, nor should they be dismissed as "not being properly mentally ill." What they've done is no mean feat, and I would love to be one of those people one day. But I've also reached a point where if I have these feelings for the rest of my life, then I'm OK with that. I know how to manage them now, and they're nowhere near as insurmountable as I once thought. They're less like having King Kong on my back and more like some stones in my shoe.

While it's important to undertake all these endeavors to feel better by yourself, the most crucial thing I've learned over the years is that I am not alone. I don't have to close myself off from everyone else. You can work as hard as you possibly can, but you can't do everything by yourself. It's so important to let yourself lean on other people when you need it, to ask for a helping hand every now and then. There's no shame in that. "No man is an island," said that guy once. (Again, thanks degree.)

Learning that I'm not alone has been more than just building a support network; it's also realizing just how many people experience mental illness, that there are others who've gotten through days as bad as yours, too, and that there's this invisible but powerful thread that connects us all.

That's what these comics have given me. When I first started them, I didn't expect anything more than a few laughs from my friends. To see so many people enjoy them, comment on how much they can relate to them, and share what they've gone through is more meaningful to me than I can ever convey. If you are reading this and you've found that you identify with even one page of it, then thank you. This book is for you. You have helped me—are helping me even now—feel less alone and accept that even if I have the worst day of my life, it's still just one day that time will carry me through to the new one waiting at the end of it.

I've said several times throughout this book that improvement is not a linear process. It's a squiggly line with countless dips and rises. It's the ten million baby steps that lead you through the desert. Some days you'll be on top of the world, and others you'll scream with frustration because you knocked a drink over and you feel like a big, dumb idiot. Eventually, you'll realize that the good days are starting to outnumber the bad. Even if you do still have terrible moments, it's OK. Their edges will soften, maybe barely perceptibly, but they will. Whatever you've been through, you've gotten through it. Nothing can ever take that away. There'll always be that part of you that's come out the other side of something awful; it may be scathed, and it may have changed you, but it's there. No matter how deep it's buried within you, it's there, and even on days when you feel your worst, it's still proof that you are so very strong. If there are days when that part isn't rooting for you, then I'll cheer on its behalf.

Just take things as they come. You've finished this book, and now your next steps are up to you. Your story is still going, and it will be amazing.

ACKNOWLEDGMENTS

Thank you to Phil, Imogen, Anna, Georgia, Lauren, and all the other wonderful people at Unbound who made this book a reality.

A special big thank you to Katherine, who did an immaculate job of wading through my gibberish and shaping it into something readable.

All my love and thanks to Mum, Dad, Ezra, Cort, Rhi, Eddie, Erica, Stefan, family members, friends, and colleagues, who patiently listened to me prattle on about this for months on end and never wavered in their support.

Finally, thank you to everyone who has ever liked, shared, or commented on one of my silly comics on social media. You made this happen! This book is for you! I love ya lots.

A NOTE ON THE AUTHOR

Chuck Mullin is a twentysomething Londoner who is full of anxiety and has a love of pigeons. She likes to combine the two of these things into comics that depict life with mental illness.

You can find Chuck @charlubby on Twitter and @chuckdrawsthings on Instagram.